Library of
Davidson College

Alternative Directions
in Economic Policy

Alternative Directions in Economic Policy

EDITED BY

Frank J. Bonello and
Thomas R. Swartz

UNIVERSITY OF NOTRE DAME PRESS
NOTRE DAME – LONDON

338.973
A466

Copyright © 1978 by
University of Notre Dame Press
Notre Dame, Indiana 46556

"Crisis in the American Economy" (originally titled "Beyond Pragmatism in the American Economy") is published by permission of Transaction Inc. from *Society* v. 14, no. 3. Copyright © 1977 by Transaction Inc.

Library of Congress Cataloging in Publication Data

Main entry under title:

Alternative directions in economic policy.

   Includes bibliographical references.
   1. United States—Economic policy—1945—
—Addresses, essays, lectures. 2. United States—
Economic conditions—1945—   —Addresses, essays,
lectures. I. Bonello, Frank J. II. Swartz, Thomas R.
HC106.5.A59398   338.973   77-17422
ISBN 0-268-00584-2
ISBN 0-268-00585-0 pbk. 80-5682

Manufactured in the United States of America

Contents

Foreword	vii
Preface	xi
Acknowledgments	xvii
Macroeconomic Performance and Policy: A Thirty-Year Perspective Frank J. Bonello and Thomas R. Swartz	1
Crisis in the American Economy Charles K. Wilber and Kenneth P. Jameson	34
Understanding Inflation Lawrence R. Klein	62
Business and Government: The Changing Relationship Murray L. Weidenbaum	78
The Social Control of Economic Power Willard F. Mueller	125
The Great Recession of the 1970s: Domestic and International Considerations Leonard A. Rapping	152
Contributors	181

Foreword

FELIX FRANKFURTER, the great Supreme Court justice, once noted that economics is "the very foundation of social and moral well being." If his insight was relevant for the 1940s it is even more relevant today. The massive income generated by the U.S. economy, if wisely and equitably distributed, can help humankind, both here and abroad, to achieve full human potential. But if our economy falters, or if its massive income is siphoned off for the benefit of a few, the great social and moral leadership role which the U.S. could play will be severely restricted and perhaps totally lost to humankind.

Just a few years ago, economists assured us that the booms and busts of the business cycle were economic history. Unemployment could be held below 4 percent. Inflation was not a concern. Real economic growth would continue indefinitely. Domestic poverty eventually would be eliminated. But then came the recession-depression of the 1970s. No longer were high school and college graduates assured of employment. Inflation ravaged the economy, preying upon those least able to cope: the old, the unemployed, the poor. Economic growth was brought to a jarring halt. Without a growing, vibrant economy, more and more families experienced the despair of poverty.

These were only the outward signs of a faltering economy. More important subtle changes were occurring. Many political and business leaders and their economic advisors outlined programs and policies designed to reduce unemployment and inflation; but the goals were now 6 percent unemployment and 6 percent inflation. As the wage earner's pocketbook thinned, school bond referendums were increasingly defeated, municipal budgets severely restricted, concern for the poor faded, and a new mood of isolationism began to appear.

Perhaps most distressing to the lay person is the fact that, as one reads this book, the anxiety and fears of the professional economists are all to evident. They, too, see changes. Gone is the optimism of the Kennedy years. Gone is the universal confidence that the economy can be fine-tuned. Gone is the bold policy prescription for a bright future. Instead, one finds pessimism, indecision, and conflicting economic policy. The nation's leading public-policy economists perceive fundamental problems in our economic system: the coexistence of inflation and unemployment, the overregulation of private business, the growing economic power of corporations, and the inherent weaknesses of a mixed market system.

We have violated our environment, failed to recognize that the supply of basic resources is finite, been insensitive to the effects of economic growth, and now are on the verge of change, a change not born of choice but a change forced by necessity. Any change in the course that we have pursued for the past two hundred years will dramatically alter the basic institutions in which we have placed our confidence. If we are to be effective participants in the new institutions that may eventually evolve—indeed, if we are to exercise our fundamental democratic right properly in shaping these institutions—we must understand the economist's concerns and the economist's proposed policy. As John Kenneth Galbraith maintains: "One of the greatest pieces of economic wisdom is to know what you do not know." If you know what you do not know, you can set about correcting the deficiency. However, if you remain uninformed, others will set policy which is based on their values and priorities; values and priorities which may be totally alien to yours.

Are the concerns that are raised in this book real for our generation? Consider the implications of the problems unearthed by these economists. Professors Wilber and Jameson detail the competing economic theories that are used to explain the apparent "crisis" confronting the American economy. Their essay, which provides an introduction to the papers of our visiting economists, concludes that the "American economy will continue to lurch from crisis to crisis unless some fundamental changes are made in our economic institutions." The nature of this "crisis" and the institutional changes implied in proposed solutions are then considered by our visitors.

Professor Klein addresses the issue of inflation. He traces one root cause of our current inflation to the traditional adversary relationship between management and labor. This is a relationship where both sides attempt to maximize their well-being and, in the process, drive production costs and prices upward. Professor Klein suggests that a "fair-shares policy" be accepted and be implemented through some form of a "social compact" between management and labor. This social compact or social contract would replace the adversary mode of negotiation with a cooperative model.

Professor Weidenbaum's concern centers upon the growing involvement and interference of the public sector in the affairs of the business sector. He would temper the growing influence of governmental commissions and agencies, particularly those concerned with consumerism, occupational safety and health, employment opportunities, and the environment. Although sympathetic with these concerns, Professor Weidenbaum pleads for greater economic justification of individual actions, a coordination of regulatory agencies, and a renewed dependency upon the market and management decision making to redress these problems.

Our third visiting economist, Professor Willard Mueller, is also concerned with the relationship between the business sector and the public sector, but his concern focuses upon the lack of forceful involvement, rather than overinvolvement. Professor Mueller sees the almost totally unconstrained growth of individual corporations and the implied concentration of economic power as a threat to individual freedom. He postulates four alternative policies, each of which would substantially alter the economic system: (1) "abandon the field" to large corporate interests, (2) "embrace a comprehensive system of controls," (3) "nationalize," and (4) through intensified governmental action, make the existing institutions work.

The last perspective, offered by Professor Leonard Rapping, anticipates sweeping changes in our society. He maintains that the "increasing concentration of economic power" precludes the successful guidance of Adam Smith's "invisible hand." He gives "faint hope" to the development of a "social contract" and anticipates a day when "central planning" will direct the flow of economic activity.

We do not know what lies ahead for this generation of young adults. We *do* know that out of change, good and evil can spring. If the lessons of history have been learned, this generation will seize the opportunity for good. They will ensure that the fundamental Judeo-Christian concern for human rights will permeate the new institutions that will slowly but inexorably evolve.

> Reverend Theodore M. Hesburgh, C.S.C.
> President
> University of Notre Dame

Preface

> *The instability of the economy is equalled only by the instability of economists.*
>
> John H. Williams
> *New York Times*, June 2, 1956

WILLIAMS'S COMMENT may once again ring true. But many economists, particularly those who wrote, advised, practiced, and taught in the 1960s, have been reluctant to re-embrace his observation. Economists have tasted the power and prestige associated with that remarkable decade of the 1960s. The ability to control the economy at long last had been achieved! Presidents, congressmen, business leaders, mayors—all sought their advice. Academic colleagues from other disciplines marveled at their models. Newspapers learned their jargon. Elementary school children were taught supply and demand. What magnificent years!

The 1960s were indeed magnificent years. However, unobserved phenomena were preparing to make their presence known. The market system and what was expected from that system had changed. We were no longer willing to accept "market failures." Our attempts to provide "guns and butter" proved to be foolhardy. Weather conditions and the resulting food shortages across the world heightened our sensitivity toward the Third World. The Club of Rome shocked us with its neo-Malthusian predictions. OPEC flexed its muscles and set off a chain reaction in international trade relationships. And then the calamity of all calamities: the U.S. and most of the world went into a recession so severe that many referred to it as a mini-depression.

What went wrong and what institutional adjustments are proposed by economists is the subject of this book. The economics department of the University of Notre Dame, taking the lead from Professors Wilber and Jameson, sought out economists who reflect the theoretical camps discussed in their paper, "Crisis in the American Economy." (Their paper, which in an abridged form appeared in *Society/Transaction*,[1] isolates four distinct groups of conflicting economic theories: the "Grand Neoclassical Synthesis," Conservative Economic Individualism, Institutional Economics, and Unreconstructed Keynesianism or Marxism.) The department called upon the most articulate and respected American economists to share their concerns and prognoses with us. These economists, who were drawn from the principal theoretical camps of the profession, were invited to interact with our students to present formal and informal seminars, to attend a number of ongoing courses, and to present a formal paper on "New Directions in Public Policy." Four major addresses constitute the major portions of this book.

Representing the "grand neoclassical synthesis" is Professor Lawrence R. Klein, Benjamin Franklin Professor of Economics at the University of Pennsylvania. Professor Klein focuses upon the extraordinary inflation which has gripped the world economy during the 1970s. He differentiates six major types of inflation, indicates the international implications of inflation, and highlights the

1. Charles K. Wilber and Kenneth P. Jameson, "Beyond Pragmatism in the American Economy," *Society/Transaction* (March/April 1977), pp. 79-83.

impact of inflation on various demographic groups. Most importantly, however, Professor Klein considers the relationship of inflation and economic activity. He finds that there is no consistent empirical relationship between inflation and unemployment. Both inflation and unemployment are part of the larger economic system and each is driven by an independent set of exogenous variables. Thus he rejects the universal application of the traditional Phillips curve tradeoff, that is, inflation as measured by money-wage changes is inversely related to unemployment, and the Alan Greenspan view that inflation as measured by money-wage changes is positively related to unemployment. He concludes that the occurence of simultaneous high unemployment rates and inflation rates is explained by the types of inflation the world has experienced—non-demand-pull inflation—and the structural changes that have caused these inflationary pressures.

Professor Klein remains a Keynesian. Stable prices, high levels of employment, and economic growth can be achieved simultaneously by reestablishing an "incomes policy," enforced by a "social contract," and by correcting for the structural problems—lack of competition, job training, and large-scale capital investment—that have crept into the economy.

Professor Murray L. Weidenbaum, Director of the Center for the Study of American Business at Washington University, is an articulate champion of "conservative economic individualism." He is distressed and alarmed by the incursion of the public sector into the private decision-making realm of the business sector. He details the growing pervasiveness of the new regulators: the Consumer Product Safety Commission, the Occupational Safety and Health Administration, the Equal Employment

Opportunity Commission, and the Environmental Protection Agency; documents the economic costs of their activities; and offers policies to reform the regulatory process. Permeating his comments is a plea to return to a free market—a market which is directed by individual decision making and monitored by—not controlled by—the public sector.

The structuralist or institutional school of economics is embodied in the comments of Professor Willard F. Mueller, William F. Vilas Research Professor of Agricultural Economics at the University of Wisconsin. Professor Mueller examines the concentration of economic power within our corporate sector. As an antitrust theorist and practitioner, he warns the reader that the competitive underpinnings of our economy are being eroded by the unrestrained growth of a number of large corporations. With this concern in mind, Professor Mueller establishes an "agenda for reforms," which includes improving the effectiveness of antitrust policy, the introduction of an incomes policy with voluntary or mandatory price, profit and wage restraints, and the regulation of multinational corporations.

Although Professor Mueller dwells upon the abuses of corporate power in our business sector, he emphasizes that "most industries are still quite competitive." Thus, if new initiatives and policies can be implemented to reshape the "structure" of the few corporations which abuse their position of power, the numerous benefits of a market system can continue to flow to the economic community.

The concluding chapter is by Professor Leonard A. Rapping, professor of economics at the University of Massachusetts. Professor Rapping's views are shared by many economists of the "unreconstructed Keynesian or Marxist" persuasion. Professor Rapping's concern is also for the enormous concentration of economic power in the U.S. and abroad. However, unlike Professor Mueller, he considers this power to be a continuing reality for our economic society. Indeed, Professor Rapping traces many of our current and past economic ills to the struggle that large financial and industrial corporations have experienced in maintaining and exercising their power. The explicit recognition of the permanency of this economic power generates distinctly different perceptions of the fundamental operation of our economy and its likely course for the future.

Central planning, both here and abroad, is forecast. However, for Professor Rapping central planning is greatly influenced by the "giant banks" and "giant conglomerate corporations." These power brokers, although not monolithic or without internal dissension, will provide the economic muscle to discipline any "social contract" which may evolve, a contract which these same interests are intimately involved in articulating. Likewise, in the international sphere, concentrated corporate power in the U.S., Western Europe, and Japan will exercise its power position for its own self-interest which may lead to "a new epoch of capitalist prosperity—perhaps under fascism."

While the papers in this collection reflect widely divergent views, considerable attention is paid to the impact of U.S. policy on the world economy and the impact of worldwide developments on U.S. economic policy. The U.S. does not exist in a vacuum. The growing recognition of this interdependency and its immediate implications were explicitly stated by Fr. Theodore Hesburgh in his observation that

> a new vision is needed if man is to create on earth the beauty that this planet manifests from afar. The vision must be one of social justice, of the interdependence of all mankind. Unless the equality, the oneness, and the common dignity of mankind pervade the vision,

the only future of this planet is violence and destruction on an ever increasing scale—a crescendo of inhumanity that can only result in total destruction.[2]

But before we release the reader to examine in detail the views of these economists, we must set the stage. We have provided the uninitiated with a brief review of the post–World War II U.S. economy. We open this first chapter with a quotation from the Employment Act of 1946— the first formal U.S. commitment to broad economic goals. The success and failure of the U.S. in achieving these and other economic goals, and the policy instruments used to achieve these ends, are then considered. Hopefully, this historical information will bring the reader up to date and provide the necessary background to appreciate the significance of *Alternative Directions in Economic Policy*.

2. Theodore M. Hesburgh, C.S.C., *The Humane Imperative; A Challenge for the Year 2000* (New Haven: Yale University Press, 1974), p. 103.

Acknowledgments

THE EDITORS ARE grateful for the enthusiastic participation of our principal contributors: Lawrence R. Klein, Willard F. Mueller, Leonard A. Rapping, and Murray L. Weidenbaum. In addition to their formal papers, which form the substance of this book, they spent many, many hours with our students and our colleagues and, in the process, provided fresh insights into the numerous problems confronting our profession.

Special thanks go to Churck Wilber, our departmental chairman, and Ken Jameson, our energetic colleague. Not only did they provide the manuscript that formed the outline for this book, they contributed generously of their time and effort to make our lecture series a success. Of course, our whole adventure into *Alternative Directions* would not have been possible without the generous support of the University of Notre Dame.

TRS and FJB

Alternative Directions
in Economic Policy

Macroeconomic Performance and Policy: A Thirty-Year Perspective

Frank J. Bonello and Thomas R. Swartz

THE EMPLOYMENT ACT of 1946 is generally regarded as the cornerstone of U.S. macroeconomic policy. As a declaration of policy, section 2 states:

> The Congress hereby declares that it is the continuing policy and responsibility of the Federal Government to use all practical means consistent with its needs and obligations and other essential considerations of national policy, with the assistance and cooperation of industry, agriculture, labor, and State and local governments, to coordinate and utilize all its plans, functions, and resources for the purpose of creating and maintaining, in a manner calculated to foster and promote free competitive enterprise and the general welfare, conditions under which there will be afforded useful employment opportunities, including self-employment, for those able, willing, and seeking to work, and to promote maximum employment, production, and purchasing power. [U.S. Code Title 15, Paragraph 1021.]

It is important to note several differences between the actual declaration and its practical interpretation. First, the terms "maximum employment," "production," and "purchasing power" are used instead of the more conventional terms "full employment," "economic growth," and "price stability." Second, the pursuit of the macroeconomic objectives, as stated in section 2, is not limited to monetary and fiscal policy. Indeed, these objectives are the responsibility of state and local governments as well. Third, section 2 does not represent an unconstrained mandate for macroeconomic objectives; rather, the policies must be consistent with "free competitive enterprise and the general welfare."

Still, the practical interpretation of the Employment Act views monetary and fiscal policies as instruments to be used to achieve a sufficiently high rate of economic growth and, at the same time, low rates of unemployment and inflation. Recent statements to the effect of a crisis in both economic theory and economic policy are, to a large extent, an expression of the belief that monetary and fiscal policies cannot deliver, simultaneously, the three macroeconomic goals. Moreover, a growing number of persons believe that in terms of promoting goal performance, the efficacy of monetary and fiscal policies has been decreasing. As a consequence, suggestions for improved economic performace range from the extreme of elimination of monetary and fiscal policies to the opposite extreme of a new social order.

The purpose of this essay is not to review the alternative suggestions or to propose and support our own particular view. That is the object of the other essays in this book. Rather, this chapter will attempt to establish a historical perspective by reviewing U.S. macroeconomic performance and policies since 1947. Hopefully, this will allow the reader to better appreciate the extent of current problems as well as the alternative views on the solutions of these problems.

U.S. Economic Performance

Economic Growth

From a conceptual perspective, a society experiences economic growth if the economic well-being of its members, on balance, increases. Real Gross National Product (RGNP), although it does not closely correspond to the conceptual measure, is the standard used to gauge economic growth. An increase in RGNP reflects an increase in the production of goods and services, that is, an increase in the volume of productive activity. It ignores such questions as the distribution and composition of the increased output, the increase in pollution and work effort which may have been required to expand output, and the rate of population growth. Because of these omissions, RGNP departs from the ideal measure of growth. RGNP as a measure of economic growth reflects a material perspective and can only be justified on the premise that it is somewhat less ambiguous than measures which attempt to incorporate certain nonmaterial perspectives and certain distributional and compositional considerations.

Once we recognize the limits of RGNP as a measure of economic growth, a basic question remains: Why is economic growth a goal? The answer is more complex today than it was in 1946. The standard response is that individuals prefer—assuming everything else is constant—more than less, and therefore an increase in the output of goods and services implies increasing levels of well-being for individuals and the larger society alike. Additionally, economic growth supports the goal of full employment; that is, increases in RGNP must be sufficiently large to absorb an expanding and increasingly productive labor force, otherwise rising unemployment will result. In this context, decreases in RGNP or negative rates of change are undesirable and large positive changes (and rates) are preferred to smaller positive changes. However, recent years have witnessed many attacks upon the desirability of economic growth. These attacks rest on the proposition that the positive impact of increased material abundance may be more than offset by certain negative and usually ignored side effects. If the hidden costs of the growth process, such as environmental damage and reduction in the stock of nonrenewable resources, are considered, society may be better off to trade increased output for "no growth" or "slow growth." Objections to increasing RGNP take this form and suggest that there is a need for a broader, more comprehensive measure of society's well-being. These considerations have had an effect, and most economists agree that a wider perception of well-being and growth is desirable. Unfortunately, agreeing that RGNP is too narrow a perception does not mean that an alternative, generally accepted measure is immediately available.

Column 2 of table 1 presents the yearly percentage changes in RGNP over the 1947-76 period, and these data indicate that the U.S. economy has been unable to achieve stable and sustained economic growth. The period begins with a negative percentage, an actual decrease in the volume of goods and services produced. Over the 30-year period, six negative growth episodes occur: 1947, 1954, 1958, 1970, 1974, and 1975. Even during the years of positive growth, there is substantial variation, from a low of 0.6% in 1949 to a high of 8.7% in 1950, the first year of the Korean conflict.

These data can also be used to indicate why the last few years have been considered a period of crisis. Consider the following:

1. Only in the 1970s have there been two consecutive years of negative growth;

TABLE 1

U.S. MACROECONOMIC PERFORMANCE—1947-76

Year	Percentage Change in Constant Dollar, Gross National Product	Unemployment Rate	Percentage Change in Consumer Price Index (December to December Change)
1947	-1.6	3.9	N.A.
1948	4.1	3.8	2.7
1949	0.6	5.9	-1.8
1950	8.7	5.3	5.8
1951	8.1	3.3	5.9
1952	3.8	3.0	0.9
1953	3.9	2.9	0.6
1954	-1.3	5.5	-0.5
1955	6.7	4.4	0.4
1956	2.1	4.1	2.9
1957	1.8	4.3	3.0
1958	-0.2	6.8	1.8
1959	6.0	5.5	1.5
1960	2.3	5.5	1.5
1961	2.5	6.7	0.7
1962	5.8	5.5	1.2
1963	4.0	5.7	1.6
1964	5.3	5.2	1.2
1965	5.9	4.5	1.9
1966	5.9	3.8	3.4
1967	2.7	3.8	3.0
1968	4.4	3.6	4.7
1969	2.6	3.5	6.1
1970	-0.3	4.9	5.5
1971	3.0	5.9	3.4
1972	5.7	5.6	3.4
1973	5.5	4.9	8.8
1974	-1.4	5.6	12.2
1975	-1.3	8.5	7.0
1976	6.0	7.7	4.8

Source: 1947-73 from *1976 Economic Report of the President* (Washington: Government Printing Office, 1976) and 1974-76 from *Economic Indicators,* July, 1977 (Washington: Government Printing Office).

2. Half of the yearly negative growth rates of the last 30 years have been crowded into the last seven years.

Society's sensitivity toward the current situation was heightened by the fact that the poor growth record for the 1970s followed a period (1959-69) which saw only positive growth rates and which led some to believe that instability was a thing of the past. Reworded, performance during the 1960s was quite remarkable and many economists came to believe that the efficacy of monetary and fiscal policies had been proved. The record of the 1970s suggests that this conclusion was premature. Indeed, it can only be concluded that either appropriate policies were not enacted, or if they were enacted, they were poorly executed, or that the problems were not amenable to conventional monetary and fiscal policies.

Full Employment

Section 2 of the Employment Act also refers to "maximum employment." As previously indicated, this is interpreted as a call for full employment. From a conceptual perspective, a state of full employment would exist when, at prevailing wage rates, all those seeking work are able to secure the type of employment they desire. But just as the conventional measure of economic growth, RGNP, does not closely correspond to the conceptual definition, the conventional gauge for the employment objective does not closely match the conceptual definition.

More specifically, the state of the economy in terms of employment is measured by the unemployment rate. This is the percentage of the civilian noninstitutional population, age 16 and older, who are able and willing to work but cannot find work. If an individual does not have a job and is not looking for work, that individual is not in the labor force and therefore, for definitional purposes, is neither employed nor unemployed.

Without reproducing the official definitions, an "employed" person can be described as an individual who has a job while an "unemployed" person is someone who doesn't have a job and is actively looking for work. Note again that a person who doesn't have a job but isn't actively looking for work is not counted among the unemployed.

The definitions, as might be expected, are subject to a number of criticisms. The following is a short list of the more important criticisms:

1. The unemployment rate ignores the discouraged worker—the individual who doesn't have a job and who has given up looking for work because previous job searches have gone unrewarded;
2. The employed category includes individuals who work part time even though they desire to work full time;
3. The employed category includes individuals who are working at jobs that do not match the kind of work for which they are qualified;
4. The employed category includes certain individuals who have a job but were not at work during the survey period, because "they were temporarily absent because of labor dispute, bad weather or because they were taking time off for various other reasons."

Just as there is controversy over the meaning of employed and unemployed, there is disagreement as to which level of the unemployment rate should be considered as indicative of full employment. To some, full employment is represented by an unemployment rate of 3.5%, to others it means an unemployment rate of 6%. All would agree that the definition of full employment does not mean a zero unemployment rate since some persons will always be "between jobs."

Before turning to the performance of the U.S. economy with respect to its employment objective, we must raise the question of why full employment is a goal of national economy policy. There are several answers to this question, but two seem most relevant to the current discussion. First, the full-employment objective is compatible with and complementary to the economic growth objective. Very simply, increasing employment is a means of increasing the output of goods and services. Second, to the extent that persons are unemployed, human resources are wasted. After all, an individual is not like a natural resource, such as coal. If a natural resource is not used, it will be available for future generations, but an individual who is unable to use his or her skills and talents today will be unable to contribute to the well-being of future generations.

Column 3 of table 1 displays the annual unemployment rates observed over the last 30 years. Examination of these data yields a number of interesting points. First, unemployment rates less than 4% are the exception rather than the rule; rates less than 4% are observed in only nine of the 30 years. Second, low unemployment rates tend to be associated with war years: the low rates of 1951 and 1952 with the Korean War and the low rates of 1966-69 with the Vietnam War. This tendency can be traced, in part, to the fact that war years represent periods when government demand for goods and services (military hardware) is quite high and, at the same time, young men are forced into military service, which absorbs some of the unemployed and/or creates job opportunities for those who are not drafted.

The third point concerns the contention that the 1970s represent a period of crisis. Here the protagonist might offer the following observations:

1. The seven years of the 1970s record the highest unemployment rates for any consecutive seven-year period within the last 30 years;
2. The only annual unemployment rates above 7% were

observed during the 1970s, with 8.5% in 1975 and 7.7% in 1976; and
3. In sharp contrast to the 1960s, when the unemployment rate trended downward (only in two of ten years did the unemployment rate increase), the unemployment rate for the 1970s trends upward (there have already been three unemployment rate increases).

On this basis it can be argued that the employment experience of the 1970s is in sharp contrast to that of the 1960s. Again, it might be concluded that during the 1970s, employment policies were not pursued, or they were poorly executed, or the policies were appropriate but they failed to yield adequate employment performance.

Price Stability

The final macroeconomic goal in section 2 of the Employment Act is "maximum purchasing power," or, as it is more generally interpreted, price stability. Conceptually, the goal of price stability does not refer to constancy of all prices but to increases in certain prices that are offset by decreases in other prices, so that, on the average, prices remain unchanged. Also, price stability does not mean low prices, for price stability (the absence of average price change) can occur at either high or at low average prices. If prices on the average are rising, a condition of inflation exists, while decreasing average prices result in a condition called deflation.

Measurement of average price behavior is normally accomplished by means of price indexes. The most familiar of these is the Consumer Price Index (CPI). The first step in the construction of any price index, including the CPI, is the selection of a "marketbasket," that is, the determination of those commodities whose individual prices will be aggregated to determine average price behavior. The construction of a marketbasket is actually a two-step process involving the selection of the items to be included and the appropriate "weighting" of each item. For example, the cost of tomatoes, as well as shelter, may be included in the CPI, but should an increase in the price of tomatoes be treated as equivalent to an increase in the price of shelter? Clearly not. Therefore, the price of shelter is given a greater weight; that is, it is treated as more important than the price of tomatoes.

In effect, the CPI represents the cost of the CPI marketbasket. If the prices of items in the marketbasket, on balance, increase, it will take more dollars to buy the marketbasket. Again, if the CPI increases, one can only state that prices on the average have increased; some may have gone up, some may have gone down, others remain unchanged, but on balance, the average price has increased.

The CPI is sometimes called the "cost of living." This cost of living is not fully applicable to any one consumer because any individual is unlikely to consume a marketbasket identical to that represented in the CPI. For example, the CPI marketbasket assumes that the consumption of food accounts for approximately 25% of a family's total monthly expenditures. If a given family spends more or less than this percentage, a change in the price of food, as recorded by the CPI, will not accurately reflect the change in the cost of living for that family. The same is true for each category of expenditures. If a family consumes an extraordinary amount of medical services, transportation services, clothing, etc., a price increase in one of these areas will increase its cost of living by more than the average represented by the CPI.

Other points which should be considered in evaluating the behavior of the CPI include:

1. The fact that the CPI marketbasket is revised only every eight to ten years. A marked increase in the price

of a given item may cause consumers to substitute non-CPI items for this high-price item. Thus the CPI may overstate the cost of living.
2. There are regional differences in prices as well as regional differences in expenditure patterns. Although the CPI is available for given geographic areas, most references to the CPI are to the national average. Thus an increase in the price of home-heating fuel may be an appropriate reflection of an increase in the cost of living for a family residing in a Border state but an understatement for a Northern family and an overstatement for a Southern family.
3. The CPI survey reflects the consumption patterns of a typical urban family of four persons. Rural families typically experience different consumption patterns and different price changes. Obviously, the consumption pattern of a single individual will differ significantly from that of a large family.
4. The increase in the price of a commodity may reflect a change in the quality of a commodity. Medical services are a case in point. Few would choose the medical services of the 1950s, even though the costs of those services are but a fraction of current costs. It is not clear that such quality changes are appropriately captured by the CPI.

Why should price stability be an objective of national economic policy? In responding to this question, a distinction should be drawn between anticipated and unanticipated inflation, that is, inflation which is foreseen and that which is not. An unanticipated price change is the more serious problem. If unanticipated price change occurs, income and wealth are redistributed (debtors gain and creditors lose, persons on fixed incomes lose and persons on variable incomes gain, and savers lose while nonsavers gain). This redistribution is not consistent with the economic contributions which various persons and groups have made. This is especially damaging for an economy that uses monetary incentives to allocate scarce resources.

To be more specific, a person who makes a substantial contribution in a market economy will tend to receive a substantial reward, a high income. If the real value of this income is eroded by inflation, the individual will lose the incentive for making that contribution. As a consequence, the normal operation of the market is abridged, and it is conceivable that economic activity could be severely restricted. Even in the case of anticipated price change, resources may be diverted from real productive activities to nonproductive activities which are likely to be rewarded by inflation.

The price stability record for the past 30 years is presented in column 4 of table 1. As these data indicate, inflation, rather than deflation, has historically been a problem: only in 1949 and 1954 did the CPI decrease. In addition, there have been sharp differences in rates of inflation, from a low of 0.4% in 1955 to a high of 12.2% in 1974. Finally, we again find that the performance of the economy with respect to this goal during the 1970s is unique. This last assertion rests on several points:
1. The only episode of double-digit inflation occurred during the 1970s;
2. The three highest inflation rates were all recorded since 1970;
3. The only years of the 1970s when the inflation rate was less than 4% were the two years in which there were wage and price controls; and
4. Of the nine years in which the inflation rate was above 4%, five of these years were in the 1970s.

It would again appear that the lack of price stability during the 1970s—an experience substantially different from that of previous years—was due to the abandonment

of price stability policies, the execution of improper policy, or changes in the underlying conditions, such that previously appropriate monetary and fiscal policies were unable to control the inflation rate.
As might be expected, the performance of the U.S. economy is not totally determined by the extent of economic growth, price stability, and unemployment. For this reason it is useful to consider how the U.S. economy has functioned in areas not specifically mentioned in section 2 of the Employment Act. For brevity, the discussion will be restricted to the topics of the international sector and poverty.

The International Sector

Numerous difficulties are encountered in an evaluation of the performance of the U.S. economy. This is particularly true in attempts to determine how well the U.S. has performed in its international economic role. Typically, evaluations are tied to a large number of key elements in the balance of payments, such as the net merchandise balance, balance on goods and services, balance on current account, balance on current account and long-term capital, net liquidity balance, and the official reserve transactions balance. It might also be argued that an accurate assessment of our international position requires a detailed appraisal of the commodity composition of our imports and exports as well as an evaluation of the source and destination of both commodity and capital flows.

Although full assessment of the international role played by the U.S. would take many pages, a general understanding of our past and current positions can be obtained by observing one or two of the key balance of payments accounts. Table 2 presents these data. The U.S. net balance in the merchandise account and the balance on the current account over the period 1947-76 provides a picture of our performance.

The net balance in our merchandise account is simply the difference between our merchandise exports or sales abroad and merchandise imports or purchases from abroad. Presumably, it measures the competitive ability of American industry. If domestic industry can produce more efficiently, and thus more inexpensively, than foreign industries, the U.S. will be able to sell large quantities of goods to other countries and will need to purchase relatively little from these same countries. In this case, the net export balance will be positive. Data in table 2 indicate that although there are substantial yearly variations in the net merchandise balance, a growing erosion of our competitive position begins to appear in 1968. The severity of this erosion is intensified in the 1970s, when the U.S. began to experience periods when imports exceeded exports. More specifically in the international area, the net merchandise balance implies that the 1970s are significantly different from earlier years.

A more inclusive measurement of our performance in the international sector can be obtained by examining our balance on the current account. This account includes not only merchandise transactions but also:
1. Net balance on military transactions;
2. Net investment income both private and government (income paid to Americans is equivalent to a merchandise export);
3. Net travel and transportation expenditures (a dollar spent by a foreign visitor to the U.S. is equivalent to a merchandise export); and
4. Other expenditures, including remittances and unilateral transfers (a monetary gift by an American to a foreign relative is equivalent to a merchandise import).

TABLE 2

INTERNATIONAL POSITION OF THE U.S. ECONOMY—1947–75
(in millions of dollars)

Year	Net Merchandise Balance	Balance on Current Account
1947	$10,124	$ 8,992
1948	5,708	1,993
1949	5,339	580
1950	1,122	-2,125
1951	3,067	302
1952	2,611	- 175
1953	1,437	-1,949
1954	2,576	- 321
1955	2,897	- 345
1956	4,753	1,722
1957	6,271	3,556
1958	3,462	- 5
1959	1,148	-2,138
1960	4,892	1,774
1961	5,571	3,048
1962	4,521	2,446
1963	5,224	3,188
1964	6,801	5,764
1965	4,951	4,299
1966	3,817	1,635
1967	3,800	1,273
1968	635	-1,313
1969	607	-1,956
1970	2,603	- 382
1971	-2,260	-4,041
1972	-6,416	-9,942
1973	911	- 367
1974	-5,367	-5,028
1975	9,045	11,552
1976	-9,223	-1,324

Source: 1947–69 from *1976 Economic Report of the President* and 1970–76 from *Economic Indicators* (July, 1977).

Although the data for the current account display persistent weaknesses in the early 1950s, these weaknesses pale in light of the 1970s. As the data on the merchandise account indicated, our international position began to erode in 1968 and this deteriorated position persists into the 1970s. Some general observations, gleaned from the massive data for this sector, provide further insights into the changing character of the U.S. position. First, U.S. direct investment abroad remains quite strong; but foreign direct investment in the U.S. has grown significantly in recent years. Second, the relative importance of commodity groups in U.S. exports has remained fairly constant. For example, in 1960 food and live animals accounted for 13.2% of the dollar value of American merchandise exports while machinery, transportation equipment, and other manufactured goods accounted for 53%. In 1975, these percentages were 14.6 and 58.7 respectively. Third, the relative importance of commodity groups in U.S. imports, unlike exports, has been subject to some significant changes. In 1960, food and live animals represented 19.9% of the dollar value of American merchandise imports while mineral fuels and related materials accounted for 10.5% and machinery, transportation equipment, and other manufactured goods represented 40%. In 1975, these percentages were 8.8, 27.2, and 49.9 respectively. Most of these import changes have occurred since 1973, reflecting the increasing reliance on foreign oil and the significantly higher price of this oil. Fourth and finally, the international area has felt several additional shocks beyond those associated with oil. There have been two U.S. dollar devaluations as well as a movement away from fixed exchange rates. These events suggest an unsettled situation that is distinctly different from the years that preceded the 1970s.

Poverty

Conceptually, an individual or a family is poor if its essential money needs exceed its money resources. Note that this is an absolute definition of poverty rather than a relative definition. Under the latter approach, the determination of poverty status is not based upon fixed criteria but upon the economic position of a particular individual or family relative to an "average" individual or family.

In order to operationalize an absolute standard of poverty, essential money needs and money resources must be delineated. On the needs side, the essentials include food, clothing, shelter, medical care, education, and, perhaps, other elements as well. Clearly, there is great potential for disagreement as to the interpretation of essential money needs. Given an acceptable definition of need, the actual calculation would take into account various differences between economic units, such as the size of the economic unit, its geographic location, the age distribution of its members, etc. With respect to money resources there is less room for disagreement. Money resources include earnings from all sources as well as any unearned income, wealth, access to credit, in-kind income, etc., which accrue to all the members of an economic unit.

The government statistics on poverty are based on an absolute definition of poverty. These data are based upon approximately 124 poverty thresholds (dollar figures which separate poor and nonpoor). The data incorporate many but not all the economic differences between individuals and family units. (For example, in 1975 the poverty thresholds were $5,500 for a nonfarm family of four, $4,695 for a farm family of four, $3,617 for a two-person nonfarm family whose head was between 14 and 64 years of age, and $3,237 for a two-person nonfarm family whose head was 65 or older). But not all differences can be taken into account. To the extent that health status is ignored in evaluating need, the poverty count is understated. On the resource side, wealth is ignored, as well as many nonmoney transfers such as food stamps, health-care benefits, and subsidized housing provided to poor and low-income families, thus overstating the extent of poverty. Again, we have a case where actual measurement differs from the ideal gauge.

The desirability of an antipoverty program is rarely challenged. If an economic unit is poor (given an absolute rather than an relative view of poverty), then, by definition, that economic unit is unable to satisfy its essential needs. Although this may not mean starvation, it suggests an extent of deprivation that should not go unattended.

Has the U.S. made progress against poverty? The data in table 3 indicate that after adjustments are made for inflation, there has been progress. Between 1959 (earlier data are not available on a comparable basis) and 1975, the number of poor persons decreased from 39.5 million or 22.4% of the U.S. population to 25.9 million or 12.3% of the population. The major factor that led to this reduction has been economic growth. That is, there are two ways in which poverty, defined absolutely, can be attacked: through economic growth or income redistribution. Since there has been little change in income distribution (the poorest 20% of American families received 4.8% of aggregate income in 1959 and 5.4% in 1975), the progress toward eliminating poverty must be traced to economic growth.

This is underscored when the data for the 1970s are compared to those of earlier years. The period 1960–69 witnessed a steady year-by-year decline in the number of poor persons. For the 1970s, three of the five year-to-year changes have seen an increase in the number of poor persons. Indeed, during four of the six years in the period

TABLE 3

PERSONS BELOW THE LOW-INCOME (POVERTY) LEVEL—1959-75

Year	Number of Persons (in thousands)	Percent of Total Population
1959	39,490	22.4
1960	39,851	22.2
1961	39,628	21.9
1962	38,625	21.0
1963	36,436	19.5
1964	36,055	19.0
1965	33,185	17.3
1966	30,424	15.7
1967	27,769	14.2
1968	25,389	12.8
1969	24,289	12.2
1970	25,420	12.6
1971	25,559	12.5
1972	24,460	11.9
1973	22,973	11.1
1974	24,260	11.6
1975	25,877	12.3

Source: U.S. Department of Commerce, Bureau of the Census, *Current Population Reports, Consumer Income* (series P. 60, no. 103).

1970-75 the number of poor persons was greater than in 1969. This is clearly the result of the inadequate growth and employment performance of the economy during the 1970s.

Some Conclusions about Goal Performance

This review of the performance of the American economy can be concluded by repeating the major themes which have been developed. First, each of the data series selected to reflect economic performance in the given areas represent a significant departure from the ideal measures. RGNP is less than a perfect measure of economic growth, and the data items that are used to measure the employment, price, international, and poverty conditions of the economy can be criticized in much the same way. Even with this in mind, it would appear that, in terms of each goal, the performance of the economy during the 1970s was substantially inferior to that of earlier years.

Second, the 1970s have seen a period of little growth, high unemployment, and substantial inflation, as well as witnessing deterioration in the international position of the U.S. economy and a return to a greater incidence of poverty.

The third theme concerns the cause of inferior performance. If the monetary and fiscal authorities have the ability to influence macroeconomic performance, why wasn't macro performance during the 1970s better than it actually was? To address this question, economic policy must be examined and reviewed in some detail.

Economic Policy

The previous section reviewed economic performance over the 30-year period 1947-76. This review suggested that the 1970s represent a unique period, in the sense that, with respect to the macroeconomic goals, performance in economic growth, full employment, and price stability was greatly inferior when compared to earlier years. Poor performance can also be seen in the international and poverty areas. As the previous section also suggests, this poor performance could be attributed to one of three situations regarding macroeconomic policy:

1. Macroeconomic policy was abandoned, or
2. Macroeconomic policy was not properly executed, or

3. Macroeconomic policy was undertaken, and undertaken correctly by historical criteria, but the economic environment had changed so dramatically that it rendered previously appropriate policies impotent.

This issue is addressed in this section. In particular, the record for monetary and fiscal policy over the 30-year period is examined. Special attention is given to the 1970s to determine whether macroeconomic monetary and fiscal policies were applied in the same manner as in previous years.

Fiscal Policy

Fiscal policy can be defined as the deliberate manipulation of the tax structure and/or spending programs for the purpose of promoting macroeconomic objectives. With respect to the tax structure, changes may be made in rates or in bases. For example, the federal personal income tax can be altered by changing the marginal tax rates or by changing the tax base to which these rates are applied. In terms of spending programs there are two broad alternatives: changes in government purchases of goods and services and changes in income transfers.

The difference between these two alternatives is best seen from the perspective that purchases are government expenditures for which something is obtained in exchange for the money outlay while with a transfer, no tangible good or service is obtained in return for the money expenditure. For example, when government undertakes a national defense expenditure it obtains a good or service. Therefore, national defense spending falls within the category of purchases. On the other hand, unemployment compensation and the various social security programs are representative of outlays for which no goods and services are obtained, and these, therefore, represent transfers. To repeat, fiscal policy represents changes in taxes, purchases, and/or transfers.

It must be recognized that there may also be changes in any of the three types of fiscal policy which are not the result of the deliberate actions of the policymaker. Tax collections can change without any changes in the laws which determine and define tax rates or the tax bases. For example, proceeds from the federal personal income tax increase automatically with an increase in the level of economic activity, due to the larger tax base and to individuals' moving into higher marginal tax brackets. A similar phenomenon occurs with some spending programs: unemployment benefits will fall with an increase in the level of economic activity as fewer and fewer persons need this assistance. In both cases, no legislative changes were made in the tax or expenditure programs.

Recognition of this point is a way of introducing the indicator problem, that is, the difficulty in selecting a measure which will adequately and accurately reflect changes in policy and define periods of expansionary and contractionary fiscal policy. Since taxes and government spending are influenced by the level of economic activity, the actual level of taxes and spending would be an inappropriate indicator. Instead, economists have developed the concept of the "high-employment budget" to measure taxes and spending at a given level of economic activity. That is, the economy is assumed to be at full employment and, given this assumed level of economic activity, the taxes and expenditures which would be generated by this level of economic activity are calculated. If the level of economic activity is fixed, then, presumably, the only way in which taxes and/or spending will change is through deliberate legislative action.

The overall position of the high-employment budget is taken as the basic indicator of fiscal policy. A high-employment budget surplus is generated when high-employment taxes (or, more appropriately, "receipts") are greater than high-employment expenditures. In this situation, the government withdraws more from the overall spending stream by its taxes than it puts back with its expenditures. Thus it is engaging in a "contractionary" policy. A high-employment budget deficit, on the other hand, represents a situation where high-employment taxes are less than high-employment expenditures. This is classified as "expansionary" fiscal policy because government is adding more to the aggregate spending stream than it is withdrawing. Any movement from a large high-employment budget surplus to a smaller surplus is a sign of less contraction, and movement from a large high-employment budget deficit to a smaller deficit is a sign of less expansion.

It should also be noted that expansionary policy generally is undertaken when government is attempting to stimulate economic activity, to promote economic growth, and to encourage employment. Contractionary policy is the appropriate course of action when the economy is "overheated," when the growth rate is viewed as excessive and inflation occurs at too rapid a pace.

The record of fiscal policy as reflected by the high-employment budget is presented in table 4. Is this a record of appropriate fiscal policy? To answer this question, consider the periods of high unemployment. During such periods, if fiscal policy has an immediate impact on employment, these periods should be matched by high-employment deficits. The years 1949, 1958, 1961, 1963, 1971, 1972, 1974, 1975, 1976 are years of high unemployment, each with an unemployment rate greater than 5.5%. By the simple criterion employed here, fiscal policy was properly executed during the years 1971, 1972, 1973, 1975 and 1976 and improperly executed during 1949, 1958, 1961, 1963, and 1974. Thus it would appear that, over time, the

TABLE 4

HIGH-EMPLOYMENT BUDGET—1947–76
(in billions of dollars)

Year	High-Employment Budget Receipts	High-Employment Budget Expenditures	High-Employment Budget Surplus (+) or Deficit (-)
1947	$ 45.1	$ 29.7	+$15.4
1948	45.0	34.8	+ 10.2
1949	43.1	40.3	+ 2.8
1950	46.4	40.2	+ 6.2
1951	60.0	57.9	+ 2.1
1952	66.5	71.1	− 4.6
1953	69.3	77.2	− 7.9
1954	68.5	68.9	− 0.4
1955	72.0	68.1	+ 3.9
1956	78.2	71.8	+ 6.4
1957	85.9	79.4	+ 6.5
1958	91.0	86.4	+ 4.6
1959	98.3	90.0	+ 8.3
1960	106.5	93.0	+ 13.5
1961	112.2	99.6	+ 12.6
1962	118.9	109.1	+ 9.8
1963	125.7	112.9	+ 12.8
1964	123.3	117.5	+ 5.8
1965	126.9	123.2	+ 3.7
1966	142.4	142.4	0.0
1967	151.9	163.7	− 11.8
1968	174.5	181.7	− 7.2
1969	196.2	189.0	+ 7.3
1970	205.9	203.7	+ 2.2
1971	211.5	219.3	− 7.8
1972	228.3	243.8	− 15.5
1973	260.4	265.0	− 4.6
1974	300.6	298.7	+ 1.9
1975	325.4	350.3	− 24.9
1976	361.9	383.3	− 21.4

Source: 1947–66 observations are derived from *Federal Reserve Bank of St. Louis Review* vol. 49, no. 6 (June 1967); 1967–68 are taken from *Federal Budget Trends* (March 1975); 1969–76 are taken from *Federal Budget Trends* (May 1977).

appropriateness of fiscal policy has increased. Indeed, it would appear that, at least in the context of this simple criterion and the single goal of full employment, fiscal policy has been properly executed during the 1970s.

During the periods of high employment—again assuming little or no lag in effect—there should be high-employment budget surpluses. The years 1947, 1948, 1951, 1952, 1953, 1966, 1967, 1968, 1969 are such years, each with an unemployment rate of less than 4%. In the early years (1947, 1948, 1951) there were high-employment surpluses, but for the other six years, only one shows a surplus—1969. These cases suggest that for these periods of accelerated economic activity, fiscal policy has become increasing inappropriate. Clearly, this conclusion does not extend to the 1970s, for, as yet, periods of low unemployment have not occurred.

But the appropriateness of fiscal policy need not be judged simply by the relationship between the unemployment rate and the high-employment budget. Instead, the relationship between inflation rates and the high-employment budget can be considered. With this relationship, high (low) inflation rates should be matched by high-employment budget surpluses (deficits). (Again, this criterion assumes away the problems of lags.) Also note that periods of high inflation may also be periods of low unemployment—that there may be an inverse relationship between these two phenomena, as suggested by Phillips curve analysis. In such cases, contractionary fiscal policy is appropriate in terms of both goals. If high inflation occurs in a period of high unemployment, either contractionary or expansionary policy would be appropriate, depending on which problem is considered more important.

If we focus on periods of rapid inflation—periods where the percentage change in the CPI is greater than

4%—no consistent pattern emerges. Some of these years—1950, 1951, 1969, 1970, 1974—had high-employment surpluses, while the others—1968, 1973, 1975, and 1976—had high-employment deficits. These latter cases would be judged as instances of improper fiscal policy, unless it is recalled that, at least in 1973, 1975 and 1976, substantial unemployment also existed.

For the sake of brevity, the periods of deflation and low inflation will not be analyzed here. Rather, the need is for some summary statement regarding the appropriateness of fiscal policy over the three-decade period and the 1970s. For the overall period, fiscal policy does not earn much applause. There are numerous years with little inflation, high unemployment, and contractionary fiscal policy, of which 1958 is perhaps the best example. There are a few years of inflation, low unemployment, and expasionary fiscal policy, of which 1967 is indicative. These examples are the evidence for the general case of the inappropriateness of fiscal policy. As for the 1970s, fiscal policy seems more appropriate, but this assessment requires that unemployment be considered a more severe problem than inflation. It should be remembered that these statements assume that the "high-employment budget" is the proper indicator of fiscal policy and that lags and the proper size of fiscal actions have been ignored.

Monetary Policy

Monetary policy, simply conceived, represents changes in the money supply. Of course, variations in the money supply, however defined, can be expected to generate a wide spectrum of effects before impinging on the goal variables of growth, employment, and price stability. As a consequence, there is difficulty in selecting an appropriate indicator for monetary policy. Even if the choice were limited to the money supply, a decision has to be made between alternative definitions of the money supply as well as the selection of an appropriate dimension: level, change, rates of change, etc. However, many argue that the appropriate indicator may not be found among alternative definitions and dimensions of the money supply but may be better represented by bank credit, some measure of reserves, or even interest rates. Rather than attempt to settle this controversy, monetary policy is evaluated here in terms of only two possible indicators. The first is percentage change in the narrowly defined money stock—changes in the volume of coins, currency, and demand deposits or checking deposits at commercial banks. The second is the level of the long-term interest rate—the Aaa corporate bond rate.

The money stock is generally assumed to be under the control of the monetary authority, the Federal Reserve System (the Fed). By using its instruments of general credit control—open market operations, the discount rate, and legal reserve requirements—the Fed can generate changes in the money supply. It can—assuming everything else remains constant—cause the money supply to rise or fall, and to rise and fall at varying rates. Normally, if the Fed wishes to adopt a neutral stance, it will set the growth rate in the money supply to match the long-term growth rate in RGNP. In order to stimulate economic activity, that is, to engage in expansionary monetary policy, the growth rate of the money supply will be made greater than the long-term growth rate in RGNP. Contractionary monetary policy can be viewed as the opposite situation, where the growth rate of the money supply is made less than the output growth rate. The classification of policy can be generalized somewhat further by asserting that decreases in the growth rate of money are movements toward less stimulus and more restraint while increases imply more stimulus and less restraint.

The second indicator is the long-term corporate interest rate. In this case the basic logic is that, before an increase in the money supply can have an expansionary impact on the economy, the increase in the money supply must be translated into a decrease in the market rate of interest. That is, an increase in the money supply, no matter how large, will not promote an increase in the pace of economic activity unless it first causes a fall in the interest rate. To be more specific, when interest rates are used as an indicator of monetary policy, falling interest rates represent expansionary policy while rising interest rates are interpreted as contractionary policy.

Note that with both indicators, other economic forces, totally apart from the deliberate actions of the Fed, have not been eliminated. Thus, unlike the case of the high-employment budget, economic activity may affect both the money supply and the interest rate, and thus the changes in these variables may be the result of changes in monetary policy and/or economic activity. This represents a weakness in both indicators of monetary policy, and caution must be exercised accordingly.

Table 5 presents the record of percentage changes in the narrowly defined money supply and the long-term interest rate over the 30-year period 1947-76. If we use the former as the indicator of monetary policy, numerous swings appear in the direction of policy: there are three periods in which the growth rate in the money supply was negative, and the positive growth rates vary from 0.6% to 9.2%. The appropriateness of monetary policy can best be depicted by examining the behavior of the money supply in periods of depressed economic activity and periods of low unemployment. During periods of low unemployment, we would anticipate contractionary or low growth rates in the money supply. In years when the unemployment rate was less

TABLE 5

PERCENTAGE CHANGES IN THE MONEY SUPPLY AND LONG-TERM INTEREST RATES 1947-76

Year	Percentage Changes in the Narrowly Defined Money Supply	Aaa Corporate Bond Rate (Moody's)
1947	N.A.	2.61%
1948	-1.4%	2.82
1949	-0.2	2.66
1950	4.5	2.62
1951	5.6	2.86
1952	3.8	2.96
1953	1.1	3.20
1954	2.7	2.90
1955	2.2	3.06
1956	1.3	3.36
1957	-0.7	3.81
1958	3.8	3.79
1959	1.6	4.38
1960	0.6	4.41
1961	3.1	4.35
1962	1.5	4.33
1963	3.7	4.26
1964	4.6	4.40
1965	4.6	4.49
1966	2.4	5.13
1967	6.6	5.51
1968	7.9	6.18
1969	3.9	7.03
1970	6.1	8.04
1971	6.3	7.39
1972	9.2	7.21
1973	6.0	7.44
1974	4.7	8.57
1975	4.1	8.83
1976	6.2	8.43

Source: 1947-71 money supply observations calculated from data in *1976 Economic Report of the President*. Remaining money supply observations from *Economic Indicators* (July 1977). Interest rate observations from *1976 Economic Report of the President* and *Economic Indicators* (July 1977).

than 4% we do not find a consistent pattern of low growth rates for the money supply. For example, in 1948 the unemployment rate was 3.8% and the growth rate in the money supply was -1.4%; in 1952 the unemployment rate was 3.0% and the growth rate in the money supply was 3.8%; and in 1968 the unemployment rate was 3.6% while the growth rate in the money supply was 7.9%. In general, one could argue that contractionary monetary policy was appropriately conducted in 1948 and, perhaps, in 1952 but improperly executed in 1968.

The same inconsistency and inappropriateness of monetary policy can be found for periods which required expansionary policy. Here, proper policy would imply a coupling of high unemployment rates with high rates of monetary growth. Prior to the 1970s, the highest unemployment rates were observed during 1949 (5.9%), 1958 (6.8%), and 1961 (6.7%). In these years the growth rate in the money supply was -0.2%, 3.8%, and 3.1% respectively. If we assume that correct or appropriate monetary policy requires a high monetary growth rate to combat high unemployment—that is, there is little or no lag in the impact of the policy—these observations are evidence of an unenlightened policy.

When recourse is made to the interest-rate indicator, a somewhat different picture emerges. The behavior of the long-term interest rate does not suggest numerous swings in monetary policy but rather that monetary policy has become progressively contractionary over time. The latter conclusion follows from the steady upward movement in interest rates. Additionally, the interest-rate data, at least in the early part of these decades, do not appear to reflect policy changes in response to changing economic conditions. In 1948 the unemployment rate was 3.8% and the interest rate was 2.82%. When the unemployment rate rose to 5.9% in 1949, the interest rate only fell to 2.66%.

For 1953-54 a similar swing in the unemployment rate is observed; it rose from 2.9% to 5.5%. Again, examination of interest rates suggests a relaxation in monetary policy, but the relation was barely discernible as the interest rate fell from 3.2% to 2.9%. During the latter part of the 1960s a more consistently proper pattern for monetary policy is observed: as the unemployment rate falls from 4.5% in 1965 to 3.5% in 1969, interest rates rise from 4.49% to 7.03%. Finally, the two indicators appear to tell different stories. This is particularly true during the 1965-69 period when the interest-rate indicator implies tight or contractionary policy, which would be appropriate policy, while the growth rate in the money supply indicator suggests expansionary policy, which would be inappropriate.

Of course, the appropriateness of monetary policy can also be assessed from the perspective of price stability. Here, there should be a coupling of low rates of monetary expansion or high interest rates and high inflation; that is, periods of high inflation call for contractionary policy. In such years (1950, 1951, 1968, 1969, 1970, 1973, 1974, 1975, and 1976) there is only one instance where the growth rate in the money supply was less than 4%. If we ignore the problem of high unemployment for the latter years, this incidence suggests that monetary policy was not properly executed. In terms of the interest-rate indicator, not much assessment can be made, given the steady upward trend in interest rates.

When we focus on the 1970s, the indicator problem prevents any assessment of whether policy was appropriate during this period. The growth rate in the money supply supports the view that monetary policy was expansionary, while the interest-rate indicator behaves in a manner reflecting contractionary policy. Overall, of course, the period was one of high unemployment and extensive inflation, and thus the evaluation of policy depends on which indicator is used and whether inflation or unemployment is considered the more serious problem.

Some Conclusions about Policy Performance

Having reviewed the behavior of monetary and fiscal policy over the 30-year period and more closely during the 1970s, can we draw any conclusions about the nature of public policy during the 1970s? A somewhat tentative set of conclusions might be offered:
1. It would appear that the execution of monetary and fiscal policy in pursuit of macroeconomics goals was not abandoned.
2. It would also appear that the execution of monetary and fiscal policy was not consistent, but the mistakes in policy actions were not substantially worse than in earlier periods.
3. Therefore, the inability of policy actions to generate adequate growth, employment, and price performance seems to have been the result of a change in the economic environment which rendered previously appropriate actions inappropriate.

These conclusions can only be tentative, given the nature of the analysis. In the case of fiscal and monetary policy, the indicator problem has not been completely resolved and, therefore, definitive conclusions depend on the choice of indicators. The analysis also assumes away problems associated with lags and the possibility of variability in the lag structure. Again, this arises in part because these problems have not been resolved in the more advanced literature of the profession. For these reasons, as well as others, we must underscore the tentative nature of the conclusions.

But there is still another proviso. Assume that these tentative conclusions are correct and that during the

1970s there were changes which made conventional monetary and fiscal policies inappropriate or at least less effective than in previous periods. Does this mean that these changes are permanent? Or are they only temporary changes—or, to use economic jargon, exogenous shocks whose influences, once felt, disappear?

If the changes are permanent, how much change in policy actions is required? What are the new initiatives? What shall be their form? Their substance? Will they yield performance superior or inferior to the past? How much groping must there be, before the new policies can become effective?

The answers to these questions are not easily found, but they are of utmost importance and of sufficient difficulty that they will occupy the current and future generations of economists. Even more than that, the questions and their tentative answers must be understood by the larger society. Hopefully, the essays in this book will provide the lay person with such an understanding. Even if the essays only stimulate, and do not resolve, they have served their function.

Crisis in American Economy

Charles K. Wilber and Kenneth P. Jameson

THE LIMITS of the mixed economy have been reached. Paul Samuelson's "grand neo-classical synthesis" has come apart at the seams. The American Century, with its New Frontier and Great Society, has been mortally wounded in the jungles of Southeast Asia. Unease and foreboding stalk the land. Or so is the impression from reading the literally dozens of books and articles pouring out on the "crisis in the American economy."

In this article we attempt to review the main explanations for this alleged crisis. But before doing so, we attempt to account for the explanations by placing the current crisis in the context of American history since the 1930s.

The Historical Background

Political democracy in the United States was founded on the assumption that contending political parties shared a minimum agreement on the central economic and social structure of the nation. They might argue about high or low tariffs, gold or silver backing for the money supply, or the appropriateness of child labor laws, but these could all be fought out within the rules of the game because the central economic and social structure would not be affected by the outcome.

During the 1930s, however, this minimum agreement was threatened by the collapse of the economy into a prolonged depression. Glaring inequalities of income and wealth, widespread mortgage foreclosures, the absurdity of idle men and idle machines in the face of obvious need, and the failure of the state to take responsibility for alleviating this massive suffering came near to rending the very fabric of society. But New Deal politics and Keynesian economics rescued capitalist democracy by providing a new mainstream consensus. Potentially disruptive conflicts, such as massive income and wealth redistribution programs or major changes in the private ownership of productive property, were sidetracked by policies designed to provide minimum economic security through old-age benefits, unemployment insurance, minimum-wage laws, and guarantees of the right to organize. World War II provided the fiscal stimulus to restore full employment, and the Employment Act of 1946 gave the federal government the right and the responsibility to utilize macro-stabilization policies.

By the 1950s it was concluded that, in addition to these economic security and full-employment policies, rapid economic growth was necessary to maintain full employment and to avoid conflicts over allocation decisions. More guns and more butter was the answer, and determination of the particular composition of national output would be left to the free market. Left-Keynesians and Marxists argued that there was a difference between tanks and housing, and mink coats and X-ray machines, but they were ignored as impractical or as ideologues, since more of anything was seen as better than less.

The emphasis on economic growth required that the post–World War II economy be built upon an ever expanding per capita consumption. Thus was born the first "high mass-consumption" society. This type of society had profound implications, far beyond the economy itself. Producers had to entice consumers to spend at least at the same rate from an ever expanding personal income. Thus advertising, product differentiation, and physical and stylistic obsolesence were developed to new heights in an attempt to convince consumers that they needed the new products and had to discard the old. To accomplish this, consumption had to be turned into a virtue, and thrift—which along with God, Motherhood, and Country had been one of the Cardinal American Virtues—had to be demoted to a Crime Against Progress for consumers, while, at the same time, the absence of thrift remained as a chief explanation (along with laziness) for individual poverty. The continuous expansion of new products resulted in a sharp increase in natural resource use and a concomitant increase in environmental pollution. Potential resource shortages were dismissed with the argument that science and technology would provide timely substitutes, and pollution was dismissed as the price of progress.

In this consumer society, government was called upon to play an ever more active role. To make this ever expanding consumption possible and to pacify the poor by ensuring that they participated at least marginally in the American cornucopia, the macro-management functions of government and economic security measures had to expand dramatically. Democratic and Republican administrations alike contributed to this expansion.

To fuel this consumer economy the United States had to tap the world's resources—oil, coffee, nickel, to name but a few. As a result, foreign investments by United States corporations increased fourfold between 1945 and 1965. To protect these investments and to prevent socialism from closing off areas of the world market to our resource needs and exports, Communism, first in its Soviet then in its Chinese version, had to be opposed at all costs.[1]

Thus the United States had to maintain a worldwide military network, with all its attendant budgetary and foreign-exchange costs. This system was built after World War II, at a time when the other capitalist countries were economically prostrate and thus were no competitive threat. The United States export surplus was so large that this overseas military burden could be financed without undue stress. The resulting cost of a growing domestic military class was submerged in the pork barrel of military public works.

The "golden age" of American capitalist democracy was 1961-67. Per capita income and consumption expanded dramatically and the New Economics seemed to meet its test, for full employment and stable prices were achieved. In the euphoria of the moment, "fine-tuning" was expected to banish forever the twin evils of inflation and unemployment. In addition to successful macro-management, the period saw the launching of the Peace Corps and the War on Poverty. It was the era of the New Frontier and the Great Society. The Achilles heel of democratic capitalism—unemployment—was finally conquered and only the fainthearted glanced anxiously at the first rumblings of inflation.

Cracks began to appear in 1965; then spread through 1968, changed direction in 1969-70, and culminated in 1973-75 with the longest and deepest recession/depression since the 1930s. First came the war in Vietnam, then the revolt of the young, and inflation, pollution, food and oil shortages, and recession. Economists began to talk about a wide variety of new institutional developments that, somehow, seemed to have an ominous role in all these crises: the rise of multinational corporations, with their transfer pricing and cross-subsidization; the development of foreign multinational firms as competitors; the coincidence of the business cycles of the United States, Japan, and the Western European capitalist countries; OPEC, the oil cartel; and the apparent impotence of government.

As if this weren't enough, the whole Keynesian consensus

was shattered by the simultaneous appearance of massive unemployment and double-digit inflation—the paradigmatic manifestation of the economic "crisis." Since 1975 the crisis has changed from acute to chronic. Economists and politicians now talk hopefully of achieving 6 percent inflation and 6 percent unemployment over the next decade. Many seem willing to accept "6 and 6" as the normal state of the economy.

Out of the wreckage has sprouted a plethora of conflicting theories to explain what went wrong, and in this review we attempt to cover the most important examples. First, a battered, somewhat discredited, but rehabilitated version of Samuelson's "grand neo-classical synthesis" survives; but it now must compete with theories that would have been considered disreputable only a decade ago. This revived mainstream Keynesianism is reviewed first.

Conservative Economic Individualism, always a strong minority force in economics, gained public respectability with the elevation of William Simon, Alan Greenspan, and Murray Weidenbaum to top economic positions in the Nixon and Ford administrations. Their underlying approach is reviewed next.

A third group of economists, many from the "underworld" of Institutional Economics, have focused on changes in the institutional structure of the United States economy as the key to the current crisis. These Institutionalists and Structuralists are reviewed next.

Next, those hardy perennials, the Unreconstructed Keynesians and the Marxists, have developed new and sophisticated analyses of the apparent breakdown of capitalist society that are quite persuasive.

We conclude this review, in the final section, with an attempt to summarize our own view of the nature of the economic crisis and a brief look at the problem of choosing among the contending theories.

Revived Mainstream Keynesianism

The Keynesian analysis, which blossomed during the 1930s and which held center stage during the 1960s, was preoccupied with the problem of unemployment. When inflation was admitted as a major problem, the same fiscal and monetary policy tools were suggested as a proper response. Unemployment was caused by a deficiency of aggregate demand and could be countered if the federal government used its economic policies to increase its own spending or to induce the private sector to increase its spending. Inflation was caused by excess aggregate demand and could be countered by reversing those same economic policies to reduce spending.

In the 1960s it became apparent that the desired levels of stability in prices and in employment were not compatible. As the economy neared full employment, costs were driven up in particular markets because all markets didn't move to full capacity at the same rate. Thus prices had to rise in the industries of full capacity, resulting in inflationary pressures in the economy. Data collected and analyzed by A. W. Phillips[2] seemed to indicate that this relation between unemployment and inflation was not restricted to ranges close to full employment; indeed there seemed to be a tradeoff between inflation and unemployment at intermediate and even at high levels of unemployment. The relationship came to be called the "Phillips curve." Its implications were that there was a fixed tradeoff between inflation and unemployment: as one went down the other would go up.

As a result of this observation, the policy problem became a bit more difficult. Rather than being able to attain both goals with a high degree of success, the problem came to be the choice of the best combination of inflation and unemployment—the point on the Phillips curve which was most acceptable to society. To make matters worse, however, by the early 1970s the tradeoff had become more costly, and previously attainable combinations of inflation and unemployment were now beyond reach. The reputation of Keynesian policy manipulation was diminished. But the worst was yet to come!

As the decade of the 1970s progressed, rising prices were no longer accompanied by falling unemployment; both were rising together. The life of the Keynesian policymaker had become frustrating indeed.

Out of this generalized disorder of the Keynesian world, the economic orthodoxy of the Keynesian mainstream has attempted to salvage an acceptable explanation of the crisis, and Keynesian categories still dominate discussion of macroeconomic policy. There is still implicit in most Keynesian analysis a belief in the tradeoff between unemployment and inflation, a position which is again more likely since the two indicators no longer are rising together. Thus the problem becomes the explanation of the worsening of the tradeoff, for combinations of inflation and unemployment of 9 and 7 percent, for example, are far less favorable than the attainable combinations of the 1960s. Seemingly, the Phillips curve has shifted up, and this must be explained. Direct explanations are difficult to ferret out of the Keynesian writing.

As noted above, a major explanation for previous tradeoffs was the rigidity in prices and wages, and Keynesians seem to suggest that it is the same factors which are affecting present-day tradeoffs. Duesenberry[3] and, in this volume, Klein, for example, talk of shifting demands, of price-setting power, of labor union resistance, of government protection of the competitive sector, etc. All of these factors impart to the economy "an inflationary bias." But of course such an argument is persuasive only if it can be shown that there has been a significant intensification of the role these factors play, and such an analysis has not been forthcoming from the house of orthodoxy.

There is one change which could have caused the Phillips curve shift: the shift from an international balance of payments system, based on fixed exchange rates, to one based on floating rates. Such a system, under certain assumptions about economic policy, implies that the inflation in one country can be transmitted to another country. Thus, one shift could have been the growing influence of foreign inflationary pressures on the United States economy. However, Keynesians generally consider this factor of small importance, mainly because the size of the United States economy diminishes the possible impact of foreign inflationary impulses. For example, Duesenberry treats the problem in terms of the impact which United States inflation had on other economies rather than vice versa. Klein remains agnostic on its importance. As a result, the Keynesians leave us with a view of the economy essentially unchanged from the 1960s.

But this still does not deal with the experience of the 1970s, with both inflation and unemployment rising at the same time, nor does it deal meaningfully with the present situation of no apparent relation between the two. Some thought has been given to the earlier period, the "stagflation" of 1972-75, and in this case Keynesians look to supply-side disruptions as the basic cause of the highly unstable situation. There are a number of sources from which the supply problems came, such as worldwide weather problems which upset the global balance of food and generated a constriction in the supply of foodstuffs to the United States domestic market. Other factors, such as the heavy Russian purchases of wheat and the disappearance of anchovy off the coast of Peru, which diminished a major source of chicken feed, added to the inflationary pressures. A second disruption, of perhaps greater import, was the action of the Oil Producing and Exporting Countries (OPEC) in exercising their monopoly power by quadrupling the price of oil. This, of course, reverberated through every sector of the economy and affected supply in all areas. Some estimates[4] indicate that these factors can account for up to 60 percent of the inflation in 1973-74 and thus can be considered a major cause in explaining the instability of the period. In addition, the resulting inflation created a fiscal drag as it inflated tax revenues and as the conservative administrations of Nixon and Ford did not take the necessary offsetting expansionary policies.

Thus the Keynesians are vindicated after all, and such disruptions will not occur again if supply is stabilized and if fiscal policy is adjusted in a more correct fashion.

There is, however, one admission that there might be a serious problem with the Keynesian analysis and that any instability in the system may be much less amenable to policy control than had previously been assumed. All analysts now admit that there may be a link between instability and the expectations of suppliers and demanders. To Duesenberry and Modigliani,[5] this implies that a "shock" to the economy may take a good deal of time to work itself out, and unless it is offset immediately by fiscal policy, as seems unlikely, substantial periods of high unemployment and high inflation may be unavoidable. This is a far cry from the Keynesian smugness of the 1960s.

To get more insight into this question, we can draw upon a symposium which appeared in a volume of the *Intermountain Economic Review*,[6] with lead articles by Abba Lerner and Paul Samuelson. The articles see stagflation as a new phenomenon, highly linked to an inflationary psychology embedded in the mixed economy. The national commitment to full employment combines with the experience of the 1960s to generate expectations that reduce the ability of recessions to damp inflation. Firms expect that government will not allow a deep or lengthy recession, so there is no incentive to lower prices in order to maintain sales volume. Instead, planning for the recovery dominates and the expectation of continued inflation generates behavior that feeds inflation, as transactions are accelerated to avoid the effects of further inflation. Such analysis suggests that new stabilization policies are needed to affect expectations and thereby inflation, thus freeing monetary and fiscal policy to bring about full employment. For example, the Keller and Gray article suggests that wage–price controls can halt inflation in the short run while monetary or fiscal policy move the economy to its long-run path of growth.

However, Samuelson and Lerner are either more realistic or less inventive. Lerner accepts the expectational view of inflation, but then decides that the best we can do is live with a "natural rate of unemployment" which will fluctuate between 5 and 15 percent. In this range there will be neither runaway inflation nor economic collapse because of high unemployment! Samuelson is even less precise in his pronouncements. After indicating that the present stagflation is "rooted deep in the nature of the mixed economy," and suggesting what some of those roots might be, he forthrightly suggests that we need to find new macroeconomic policies beyond conventional monetary and fiscal mechanisms, including, it seems, short-run wage–price controls. He concludes the essay by saying "stagflation remains the Achilles heel of the modern mixed economy and the continuing challenge to professionals in economic science." Such statements would be unexceptional, if they did not emanate from the preeminent economists in the United States. One wonders who, if anybody, is minding the store of mainstream Keynesianism.

Thus we leave the Keynesian analysis in a situation of beleaguered splendor. On one side, it has little ability to analyze the apparent upward shift in the inflation–unemployment tradeoff. On the other, it must hope against hope that exogenous factors do not shock the economy, for if they do, and if they engender expectational adjustments, the stability which Keynesian analysis claims as its contribution will be unattainable and policy will be irrelevant.

Conservative Economic Individualists

One group of American economists has never believed that sustaining full employment by government actions is either possible or desirable. This group of Conservative Economic Individualists includes (among others) Alan Greenspan, William Simon, Milton Friedman, William Fellner, Herbert Stein, Gottfried Haberler, Murray Weidenbaum, and Alan Walters.[7] At the most fundamental level, they believe that the present crisis is caused by too much government intervention in the economy. As Milton Friedman recently said, "We are suffering from inflation and recession produced by government attempts to promote full employment."[8]

As a starting point, writers of this persuasion recommend abandonment of full employment as a goal of national policy. They reason as follows. Growth of government and inflation are the twin evils that threaten economic welfare and personal liberty. The establishment of full employment as a national priority generates irresistible political pressures to achieve that goal and the resultant policies set off the flames of inflation and generate an increased need for government control. Moreover, this inflation can then proceed to trigger a recession. Inflation frustrates people's plans, destroys their confidence, and creates the type of uncertainties which lead both businesses and consumers to cut back on their spending plans. The 1973-75 recession is explained in this fashion.

Conservatives also argue that the "crisis" is largely a figment of the naysayer's imagination. They claim that unemployment figures overstate the seriousness of the situation. For example, the proportion of male workers 25 and over in the work force has fallen from 60 percent in 1955 to 46 percent in 1975. Women and teenagers have less attachment to their job and thus always have higher unemployment rates. In addition, as Weidenbaum states in this volume, they argue that minimum-wage laws are the main reason for high unemployment rates among teenagers and the unskilled. Since much of the unemployment in the current crisis is concentrated in these groups, if the composition of the work force in 1975 were the same as in 1955, the unemployment rate would be appreciably less. They also argue that generous unemployment benefits make workers choosy about the jobs they will accept; so a reduction in benefits would actually reduce unemployment.

Thus the villain in all cases is the government. Conservatives like Alan Walters, Harry Johnson in his introduction to Walters, and Weidenbaum argue that the ever growing macro-management functions and social security measures of the federal government create a burgeoning bureaucracy and a politicization of economic decisions which, in turn, generate inefficiency, a loss of incentive in the private sector, and a pandering to the marginal voter by politicians with promises of ever more government programs to replace private activity. The only answer is a sharp reduction of social security programs that affect personal incentives, a transformation of macro-management into fixed rules, and the acceptance of the necessity of unemployment to cure inflation. In sum, a return to the free market, limited government, and rugged individualism is our only salvation. (Some, such as Weidenbaum, see this as utopian and hope only that government can be made more efficient by use of incentive systems.)

While such policies are presently being experimented with in situations such as Chile and Argentina, these writers tend to be pessimistic about the willingness of the American people or their political leaders to swallow the medicine they prescribe. Let us hope their pessimism is well founded.

Structuralists/Institutionalists

Such strident unanimity of analysis and conclusion does not characterize the writings of the Structuralist/Institutionalist school, analysts who see the roots of the crisis in structural developments in the United States economy. There is a wide variety of structural/institutional analyses, but it is possible to outline a basic approach that is common to them all.

This school of thought receives its name from its analytical point of departure: the economic institutions and structure of the United States economy. Developments in the basic institutions of the economy—markets, corporations, governmental structures—can substantially affect the functioning of the economy. In the particular case that is dealt with here, structural alterations can be the underlying cause of the current crisis.

Thus a structural analysis initially will focus on a particular aspect of the economy. It will be chosen as the unit of analysis for two reasons. First, the assumption will be that this institution or structure is an important influence on the functioning of the economy and, more particularly, on the performance of the economy in the areas of prices and employment. A second reason for the selection is that information will suggest that there have been changes in the institutional situation, that an alteration has occurred in the particular structure of interest whose influence is to cause or exacerbate or make less manageable the crisis which is observed. In general, Structuralists/Institutionalists paint a rather bleak picture of the crisis, but they still feel that structures can be controlled and changed by policy, and thus crisis situations can be overcome.

Of the variety of structural/institutional analyses related to the current crisis, three seem to us to be of greatest interest. John Kenneth Galbraith[9] focuses on the domestic corporation and sees its division in the twentieth century into two sectors which behave quite differently: the "market" sector of small service and manufacturing activities and the "planning" sector of the largest 1,000 business firms which are horizontally, vertically, and conglomerately integrated. Richard Barnet and Ronald Müller[10] look to somewhat the same universe, though their concentration is on those firms we now categorize as "multinationals," whose significance is seen to originate in their multinational activities. Barry Commoner[11] focuses somewhat less precisely on this group of firms for his examples of the functioning of the "economy" and its effects on the "ecosystem."

These structures are seen as the generators of inflation, unemployment, decay of public services, greater inequality, and even a certain imperial inclination. The Mueller paper in this volume presents evidence that monopoly generates inefficiency and worsens the tradeoff between inflation and unemployment. The Galbraithian planning sector, of its very nature, is prone to instability; it does not respond to signals which could equate savings and investment, thereby ensuring full employment, and prices are set internal to the firms which can pass on to the consumer all cost increases. Thus, while the market sector remains stable and self-correcting for inflation, the independence of the planning sector will inevitably lead to recurring experiences of unemployment and inflation. Also, public services will be allowed to decay because the planning sector has neither expertise nor interest in these areas.

The multinationals bring about instability in a somewhat different fashion, according to Barnet and Müller. The multinational is not necessarily unstable in its activity, but in a modern economy which must rely upon public policy to bring basic consistency to the economy, the ability of the multinational to operate on goals different from those of the nation implies that such activity may be a source of instability. In addition, increasing concentration in production, combined with the multinationals' interlocks with domestic banking and the mass media, is leading to changes in the pattern of production, the distribution of income, and the balance of power in the United States, which comes more and more to resemble a "less developed country." The potential countervailing forces to these structural changes are rendered immobile: labor is impotent, small businesses are disorganized, and the government has been captured to serve the interests of the multinationals and their domestic correspondents. Thus policy such as that which Samuelson suggests would be rendered ineffective, unless the interest of the multinational were to coincide with the interest of the nation at large.

Legal and political institutions have not kept pace with the changing techniques of accounting, finance, marketing, and production utilized by the multinational firm. The internationalization of the large corporation has magnified the old problem of secrecy and disclosure. New accounting techniques, combined with international operations, allow corporations to maintain even greater secrecy than in the past. If knowledge is a critical component of power, it is the private corporation, not the state, which is its possessor. The state simply does not have sufficient information either to regulate the multinational corporations or to make the crucial planning decisions on tax, monetary, employment, and trade policies for society. As a consequence, the corporate managers have become, by default, the "planners" for the economy. The result is that government macro-management policies are undermined, and thus the business cycle cannot be controlled. Also, the multinational corporation is becoming constantly embroiled in international intrigue, thus forcing the United States government into imperial positions.

While Commoner sees a relationship between increasing economic concentration and instability, his analysis of the basic linkages to the crisis is quite different. Based upon a number of case studies, he abstracts the generalization that a major factor facilitating concentration is the relation between profitability and energy inefficiency. Thus the nascent power of General Motors allowed it to undertake a concerted attack on urban mass transit and the electric trolley in particular, substituting the private automobile. The latter was substantially more profitable, but at the same time it was substantially less efficient in terms of its use of energy, especially if energy efficiency is measured in terms of the Second Law of Thermodynamics.[12] Thus corporate growth has been fostered by the profits which come from displacing more basic but more efficient approaches to doing work. This engenders instability when the economy reaches the limits of exploitation of the ecosystem, and it is in this conflict that Commoner finds the roots of the present-day instability in the economy.

Each writer moves from the analysis of instability to policy suggestions for confronting the crisis, suggestions which are as different as their analyses. Galbraith lays out an elaborate theory of reform of the economic system which he suggests can offset the destabilizing tendencies of the planning sector. Its cornerstone is fiscal policy, with the government raising its expenditures to ensure the satisfaction of social needs and also raising taxes, if necessary, to offset any initial inflationary impulses in this process. A second component is the abandonment of monetary policy which is seen merely as a way of punishing the market sector. And, finally, effective wage and price controls would be instituted to offset the remaining inflationary pressures in the economy. Sharply differing with Galbraith, Mueller's paper in this volume argues that an incomes policy must be supplemented by pro-competition policies.

Barnet and Müller's solution to the situation is also implicit in the analysis, though the mechanisms for attaining the solution are not specified. The basic thrust is that meaningful countervailing forces to the multinationals would offset their destabilizing effect. The suggested mechanisms are a concentrated effort to break the monopoly which buttresses these corporations, particularly in the area of knowledge and its uses, and development of national economic planning as the means to gain control over the corporations, that is, a change in the basic structures of the economy. This of course differs from Galbraith, who would attempt to manipulate given structures.

Commoner's prescription is somewhat less a part of his analysis, but certainly relates well to it. One of the implications of his treatment is that an irrationality has developed in the economy's use of the ecology because of a deviation in "production for use" and "production for exchange," where the deviation can be measured in terms of Second Law efficiencies. Such a conclusion, with its obvious Marxian analogies, implies that mere structural reforms will have little impact. Thus Commoner makes a somewhat tentative claim that the time has come to open the debate on the type of economic system which is desired, capitalist or socialist. As he puts it, the powerful (corporations) of the society have confessed their poverty, and the society which has been predicated upon further growth in material outputs, at the cost of higher Second Law inefficiency, is no longer viable, given ecological constraints. Thus mechanisms must be developed which ensure production for use, not for exchange.

Unreconstructed Keynesians and Marxists

One important result of the present disorder in the United States economy has been an increase in the amount and the range of activity devoted to more general theories of crises and cycles. In most cases this has taken the form of a rediscovery or reformulation of preexisting theoretical structures, making the literature difficult for the general reader. Nonetheless, the historical vitality of these approaches and the generally "high" level of their theory make them worth reviewing, for they are likely to have substantial importance in understanding the crisis.

The studies' point in common is that they all suggest that the North American economy is systemically given to the instability and crisis that are being experienced. Rather than a result of new structural developments, this is proof that the reforms which have been instituted to stabilize the economy can have no long-term success in the face of fundamental instability. At the most, they shift the timing of the recurring crises.

The structure of the arguments which generate these results differs substantially, though complementarities can often be found and categories in different theories can often be given common interpretation. For our purposes, however, it is useful to distinguish among three main representatives, each originating in a different preexisting theoretical structure.

The first of these is what Hyman Minsky calls the "unreconstructed Keynesians." Minsky, Al Eichner, J. A. Kregel, and Joan Robinson distinguish themselves and their belief in the fundamental instability of capitalist economies from the "Bastard Keynesians"[13] (our "Revived Mainstream Keynesians"), who have translated Keynes's fundamental belief in the instability of the capitalist system into a claim that it is "unstable except in the face of effective fiscal and monetary policy." Taking Minsky[14] as its representative can allow a basic understanding of the analytical approach. Two constructs are at the center of the Keynesian analysis: the investment process and the distribution of income between capital and labor. For Minsky, the first of these strictures provides the source of instability, with both the demand for capital assets and the supply of investment goods being unstable and, consequently, generating unstable behavior in the investment process.

Instability on the demand side originates in financial markets where uncertainties and expectations can lead to substantial swings in financing and investment demand, with a resultant impact on employment. The supply side operates through wages set in labor markets, and changes in this market can also cause instability which generally shows up on the price side, that is, inflation.

The mutual instability of these two components of the investment market generates instability in the overall economy, which suggests that only a systematic shift in the investment process can avoid the recurrent crises of the United States economy. In particular, if the entire investment process is socialized so as to negate the influence of uncertainty in investment goods prices, it would be possible to attain a stable economy. Another Keynesian concern, income distribution and economic justice, would then be solved successfully, as the investment process would operate to ensure the euthanasia of the rentier[15] and the avoidance of conspicuous consumption.

Another group of cycle theorists are the political economy analysts who draw heavily upon the work of Michael Kalecki. Good examples are Howard Wachtel and Peter Adelsheim,[16] Ray Boddy, Jim Crotty, and Leonard Rapping.[17] Kalecki's theory offers two approaches to the crisis, the first to inflation through markup pricing and the second to the cycle of output through the "political business cycle." Since Wachtel and Adelsheim examine the first, and Crotty, Boddy, and Rapping the second, it will be useful to examine both in some detail.

Markup pricing assumes that, in concentrated industries,

prices are established by firms to ensure a given return over cost. To explain the crisis from this perspective, an analyst must document the existence of market power which would allow markups, the existence of the business cycle, and, finally, must relate the two into a composite theory of cyclical inflation in the economy. In the first task, Wachtel draws upon the work of John Blair on economic concentration in the United States. His evidence on increased concentration is taken as an indicator of an increase in the importance of markup pricing since the Second World War. It is then assumed that the economy is characterized by short- or medium-term cycles. Relating markups and cycles, Wachtel and Adelsheim show that markups (and thus prices) rise in an economic upturn, but their rise is limited by competitive pressures. More important than this type of inflation is that exhibited during downturns, for in this portion of the cycle prices are raised by firms in an effort to attain a given rate of profit on a falling output, even though doing so may cause output to fall further. Thus the crisis phenomena of falling employment and rising prices are seen to result from the interaction of the cycle and the markup pricing behavior of the concentrated sector.

Crotty and Boddy provide the missing analytical step in the above analysis when they offer an explanation of the cycle as a "political business cycle." The key to their argument is the assumption that the stability of the economic system depends upon capitalist behavior, which is in turn related to the share of capital in total income. A decline in capital's share has the potential to disrupt the functioning of the economy, and therefore it will be resisted by all means, including the use of the state. Thus the question becomes the behavior of capital's share, and examination of unit labor costs over the cycle indicates that sustained full employment is incompatible with the maintenance of capital's share.

This conclusion is reached by dividing each recovery into two phases and showing that, in the later portion of the upturn, unit labor costs generally begin to rise, due to improvements in labor's bargaining power. To reverse this trend, bargaining power must be returned to capitalists, and the surest way of accomplishing this has been to engineer a recession. The resulting insecurity erodes labor's gains.

However, the current crisis presents an added complication. As a result of the misuse of the political business cycle during the 1960s (that is, allowing the expansion to continue too long) and of the increasing integration of the United States economy into the world economy, the political business cycle no longer can control the additional disruptive force of inflation. Thus recession must be combined with wage and price controls whose effect will fall primarily on wages. The situation of labor is made more acute since its gains are now limited by wage controls, as well as by politically induced business downturns.

Rapping[18] adds international finance as a significant feature to the Boddy and Crotty analysis. He argues that international financial and commercial order is difficult to achieve among unequals and, since the erosion of United States economic power after 1965, no single nation is sufficiently powerful to impose order unilaterally. The breakdown of the Bretton Woods system in August 1971 resulted in floating exchange rates, which, when coupled with recession in several major nations, pose a constant threat of an international commercial disintegration, which in turn would reinforce the domestic recessive forces.

It should be noted that the implication of the Boddy/Crotty/Rapping analysis of the crisis is far different from previous cases. Since business downturns are at the center of policy, and now must be accompanied by wage-price controls to maintain capital's share, stability is incompatible with the maintenance of the capitalist system. Rather, the struggle between labor and capital must be played out, with labor's only hope being victory in that struggle.

The final group of studies are specifically Marxist in origin, tracing their lineage back to Karl Marx. Examples are Howard Sherman, Michael Harrington, Andrew Glyn and Bob Sutcliffe, and Paul Sweezy. From a different analytical base, the latter studies reach conclusions very similar to those of Boddy and Crotty. Our treatment will concentrate on Sherman,[19] mainly because his is an extensive and relatively complete treatment of the economy in crisis, and also because his approach makes him accessible to general readers.

His starting point is a theory of business cycles which is based upon a dual profit squeeze in the recovery phase of the cycle. The squeeze comes, first of all, from the lack of effective consumer demand for products as the wage share and unit labor cost decline over the whole upturn (Boddy and Crotty found two subpatterns in the upturn). Thus profit cannot be realized. Sweezy[20] finds the main cause of "creeping stagnation" on the demand side but the main source is the lack of investment expenditures, which has to be offset by government expenditure, thus giving rise to the substantial budget deficits of recent years.

The second side of the squeeze originates in the tendency (nowhere completely explained) for raw material costs to rise in the upturn and thus for the cost of production to rise as well. A notable difference from earlier treatments is that labor power has no role in this profit erosion; indeed, theories which ascribe to labor a significant role in profit erosion are seen as "blaming the victim" for the cyclical behavior of the economy. With this theory as his base, Sherman proceeds to embellish it with references to current economic questions. Military spending is seen to represent the "political business cycle," but in this case it plays the role of the stabilizer to cycles in the private sector. The competitive sector is the area where cycles originate, rather than the monopoly sector which uses markup pricing. Stagflation has become an international phenomenon which the United States is unable to control completely at home or abroad. And expectations, innovations, inventories, etc., can exacerbate the cyclical behavior of the economy.

Sherman finally provides us with two varieties of policy. The first deals with the immediate problem of maintaining labor's gains. The fight for full-employment legislation, for nationalization of the oil industry, and against discrimination are all seen as positive steps. But in the long run, only a democratic socialist government, with a high degree of worker participation in the management of the nationalized top 1,000 firms, can assure that capital will not have its way. This two-dimensional division is useful, but we might wish that it were more directly related to the analysis of the book. Nonetheless, the coherence of Sherman's book recommends it.

Lest the reader be left with a sense of bewilderment at the diversity of these studies, it should be emphasized once again that they all agree that instability and crisis are inherent in the capitalist economy, and there will be no change until there are substantial modifications in the rules of the economic game.

Conclusion

All of these theories throw light on the reality of the economic crisis facing the United States during the 1970s. We feel that a more comprehensive analysis of the nature of this crisis can be formulated by combining and rearranging elements of those theories. What follows is our attempt to sketch the outlines of such an approach.

The starting point of our analysis is the argument that cyclical fluctuations in employment, prices, and income are inherent in the nature of a market economy. Decentralized decision making means that full-capacity production is only one possible outcome of an indefinite number. This is the insight that elevates Marx and Keynes above their peers and that must form the basis of any adequate analysis of the contemporary crisis. Marx said those fluctuations couldn't be controlled short of replacing capitalism with socialism. The "Bastard" Keynesian revolution was the belief that government fiscal and monetary policies could control those fluctuations by providing centralized decision making to counter the decentralized decision making of firms and consumers. But the history of the American economy indicates that full employment with stable prices is an aberration that occurred only during 1965–67.

The second question is why the Keynesian solution hasn't worked except during that short-lived "golden age". Briefly, we mention several factors which helped destroy the momentary triumph and which guarantee that the contemporary crisis is not simply an aberration or merely a manifestation of the anarchic nature of capitalism. The Keynesian attempt to control that elemental anarchy has created new problems that threaten to "leave the last state worse than the first."

1. The price-setting process is now highly insulated from market or policy influence, and as a result there is an inherent tendency to inflation in the economy. Markets no longer discipline price setting because of the growth in concentration and the tendency of firms to use "markup" pricing in establishing prices for their products, even in the face of policy-induced demand constriction. But in addition, the ability of the government to impose demand restraint has been lessened by the multinationalization of the corporation. Thus orthodox policy of a

Keynesian variety is at best impotent, but under markup pricing may actually encourage inflation.

2. The attempt to maintain a steady full-employment expansion inevitably undermines itself. As full employment is maintained for any length of time, profits are eroded as bargaining power shifts in favor of workers and productivity declines as labor discipline weakens without the threat of unemployment.

3. As a result of the need to provide minimum economic security for unsuccessful participants in the modern consumer society and the growth of a domestic and international war capability, there has grown up a relatively autonomous bureaucratic and military sector. Its interests are in maintaining itself and growing, and this results in the creation of another competitor for the output of the society, a competitor whose very operation can often interfere with productivity in the private sector. Thus there is a dual impact, which adds up to more inflationary pressures in the economy. In the past, this sector was able to cushion the effects of downturns to some degree, but it seems unlikely that this can be a significant factor at this point, given the present inflationary weight of the sector.

4. The attempt to build a mass-consumption society since World War II has contributed to undermining the stability of the system. The high rate of resource consumption inherent in the system has led to the beginnings of severe shortages in energy supplies and a variety of raw materials. These shortages have driven up, and will continue to drive up, costs and prices, making the maintenance of the consumer society ever more difficult. Also the polluting nature cf production will drive up costs as environmental standards are enforced. These two characteristics of production make it doubtful that economic growth can be relied on to maintain the level of employment, as it

has in the past. Yet the "growth psychology," which expects ever increasing income and consumption, will be greatly threatened by any slackening in growth; and in that event a sharply increased struggle over income shares will result.

Our conclusion, therefore, is that the American economy will continue to lurch from crisis to crisis unless some fundamental changes are made in our economic institutions. There must be a movement away from reliance on economic growth as the stabilizer and *raison d'être* of the economy. In some cases, less may be better than more. Much more vigorous policies must be devised to address the extreme inequalities of wealth and income. The power of the large corporations must be made publicly accountable through a combination of antitrust, nationalization, and national economic planning. The autonomy of the state bureaucracy must be resisted and forced to conform to broader policy concerns. But before such a comprehensive program could begin, a mass-based political party would have to gain the support of the American people. We seem to be a long way from such a goal.

We have provided yet another explanation of the crisis, but the question remains as to how one decides which of these theories is a better depiction of reality. We suggest that there is no viable "scientific" criterion. The existence of such diverse models to explain the same phenomena illustrates the extreme difficulty of empirically verifying or falsifying a theory in the social sciences. Since there are no conclusive means to verify a theory, the main issue becomes the beginning assumptions that each model builds upon. But the judgment as to which set of assumptions is more appropriate probably turns on the ideological preference of the author. Thus the reader is forced into a position of choosing among theories, relying heavily upon personal belief.

The Revived Mainstream Keynesians believed that accidental events and policy mistakes lie at the root of the present crisis and all that is needed is better policy. The Conservative Economic Individualists see too much government as the cause of the crisis, and therefore see the cure as less government. The Institutionalists, Structuralists, unreconstructed Keynesians, Marxists, and we ourselves see defects in the institutional structure of the economy as the source of the ongoing series of crises that are plaguing the economy. The recommended solutions range from mild institutional reform to the total replacement of capitalist with socialist institutions.

The choice we make will shape the future not only of the economy but of the very way we live.

NOTES

1. This does not deny that the United States opposed Communism for higher reasons—i.e., liberty—but the existence of the lower reasons strengthened its resolve.
2. A. W. Phillips, "The Relation between Unemployment and the Rate of Change in Money Wage Rates in the United Kingdom, 1861-1957," *Economica* (November 1958), pp. 283-99.
3. James A. Duesenberry, "Worldwide Inflation: A Fiscalist View," in David Meiselman and Arthur Laffer, eds., *The Phenomenon of Worldwide Inflation* (Washington: American Enterprise Institute, 1975), pp. 113-24.
4. Richard X. Chase, "The Failure of American Keynesianism," *Challenge: The Magazine of Economic Affairs* (March/April 1976), pp. 43-51.
5. Franco Modigliani, "The Monetarist Controversy or Should We Forsake Stabilization Policies?" *American Economic Review* (March 1977), pp. 1-19.
6. *Intermountain Economic Review* special issue, "Stagflation" (Fall 1975). All of the articles are of interest, but those by Keller and Grey, Lerner and Samuelson are specifically mentioned in the text.
7. William Fellner, ed., *AEI Studies on Contemporary Economic Problems* (Washington: American Enterprise Institute, 1976). All of

the essays are of interest but particularly the ones by Fellner, Phillip Cagan, Herbert Stein, Geoffrey Moore, Gottfried Haberler and Murray Weidenbaum. Also see Alan Walters, *The Politicization of Economic Decisions*, reprint paper no. 1, The International Institute for Economic Research (April 1976), and Milton Friedman, *An Economist's Protest: Columns in Political Economy* (Glen Ridge, N.J.: T. Horton, 1972).

8. Milton Friedman, "National Economic Planning," *Newsweek*, July 14, 1975, p. 71.

9. J. K. Galbraith, *Economics and the Public Purpose* (Boston: Houghton Mifflin, 1973).

10. R. J. Barnet and R. E. Müller, *Global Reach* (New York: Simon and Schuster, 1974).

11. Barry Commoner, *The Poverty of Power* (New York: Knopf, 1976).

12. Usual measures of efficiency are in terms of the First Law of Thermodynamics, which measures the amount of useful work obtained for a given input of energy. For a given "work," the Second Law calculates the relation between the actual energy input and the input which would be necessary under the most efficient conditions.

13. This does not refer to the parentage of the writers but to their implicit view of the economy in long-run growth. The term's progenitor is Joan Robinson, and it is used to differentiate these analysts from the "Left" or "unreconstructed" Keynesians.

14. H. P. Minsky, *John Maynard Keynes* (New York: Columbia University Press, 1975).

15. See J. M. Keynes, *The General Theory of Employment, Interest and Money* (London: Macmillan, 1936), chap. 24.

16. H. M. Wachtel and P. Adelsheim, *The Inflationary Impact of Unemployment: Price Markups during Postwar Recessions, 1947-70*, paper no. 1, vol. 3: *Achieving the Goals of the Employment Act of 1946-Thirtieth Anniversary Review*, Joint Economic Committee, Congress of the United States (November 3, 1976).

17. R. Boddy and J. Crotty, "Class Conflict and Macro Policy: The Political Business Cycle," *Review of Radical Political Economics* (Spring 1975), pp. 1-19. Also see J. Crotty and Leonard Rapping, "The 1975 Report of the President's Council on Economic Advisors: A Radical Critique," *American Economic Review* (December 1975), pp. 791-811.

18. See Rapping's paper in this volume.

19. H. Sherman, *Stagflation: A Radical Theory of Unemployment and Inflation* (New York: Harper & Row, 1976).

20. Paul Sweezy, "Creeping Stagnation," *Monthly Review* (January 1977), pp. 1-14.

Understanding Inflation

Lawrence R. Klein

Some Kinds of Inflation

THE MOST IMPORTANT thought that I want to bring across in this lecture is the notion that inflation is not a monolithic single-minded thing. It is, by contrast, a many-faceted thing. There are many kinds of inflation, many sources of inflation, and many different approaches to dealing with it. Inflation is not simply a matter of the relationship between rate of growth of the money supply and rate of growth of total real output; that is, the general price level is not governed solely by the quantity theory of money. It is important to know the many facets of inflation in order to deal with it properly.

Some alternative sources of inflation are:
1. Demand-pull inflation
2. Cost-push inflation
3. Grain theory of value
4. Energy theory of value
5. Administered wages and prices
6. Wartime capacity pressures

Demand-Pull Inflation

A classic definition of inflation is "a situation in which too much money (or income) is chasing too few goods." There is, in this situation, an excess of demand and, according to general reasoning, this would cause prices to rise in order to clear markets. If demand were to be restrained, the upward price pressure would lessen or disappear. Classically, this would be done through restrictive financial measures to hold money supply and credit expansion in check. In many respects, this is the policy that was followed by our monetary authorities at the Federal Reserve in order to deal with inflation during 1975. Fiscal restraint together with monetary restraint, or separately, is another policy for dealing with demand-pull inflation.

Cost-Push Inflation

High and rising costs may also be a source of inflationary pressure. If prices are set by marking up unit costs—wage, material, and capital costs—then rising costs can lead to rising prices. These pressures come from the supply side, in contrast to demand-side sources, under demand-pull inflation. Market competition is supposed to act as a restraint or barrier against cost-push inflation, but there are so many imperfections in contemporary competition that we cannot rely on this kind of structure to protect us from cost-push inflation. Fiscal and monetary restraint are not generally suitable policy tools for dealing with cost-push inflation. The promotion of competition, although this is a vague guideline, is an appropriate policy for this kind of inflation.

Grain Theory of Value

We have frequently noted that when agricultural prices are high—probably as a result of shortages—the overall price indexes are also high. We can also see the reverse phenomenon. During 1976, agricultural prices were falling or steady. This, by itself, did much to hold down the main aggregative price indexes because they have large agricultural components. Grain prices are singled out for comment because they are basic. Grains are either consumed directly (food grains) or fed to livestock (feed grains) and consumed indirectly in the form of meat or dairy products. In a country like India, with a much more serious food problem and a relatively more important agricultural sector, it may well be said that a grain theory of value plays a very large role in assessment of inflation.

Energy Theory of Value

The two most frequently cited factors in the explanation of the inflation of 1974-75 are food and fuel. Energy prices, either through fuel prices or energy conversion costs, have risen so much that they are clearly predominant in accounting for movement of the major price indexes, even though energy may be a fairly small component in total output of the economy. Energy, like food, is a specific good (a service), and its rise may be called a rise in *relative* prices, not in general or absolute prices. The fact of the matter is that the relative price rise was so large that it lifted the whole of major price indexes, and it was not simply a one-time shift in price relatives. In 1973 it was grains, followed by general commodity speculation; in 1974 it was fuel and sugar; in 1975 it was another notch in fuel and grains; in 1976 it was coffee, cocoa, and a few other products.

It is true that the inflation rate came down considerably from 1974, but it is still very much in evidence, with basic commodity price rises that roll from case to case, always showing up in the national indexes and not confined simply to relative price shifts.

Administered Wages and Prices

Cost-push inflation can take different forms. A particular form occurs as pressure from monopoly-affected prices and wage rates that are on a ratchetlike course and are held artificially high by virtue of market power. I do not mean that an absolute monopoly is involved, only that anticompetitive monopoly forces are at work to keep prices above where they might naturally be.

Connected to the general phenomenon of administered price or wage setting is the idea of a bellwether sector. Strategic price or wage bargains in steel, autos, mining, or transport may permeate other dependent sectors and set the stage for emulation, to such an extent that a whole wave of inflationary changes is triggered by a few.

It should also be pointed out that administered pricing on the inflationary side may have joint elements of demand-pull and cost-push. That is to say, a particularly high wage increase may be granted on the cost side, because a producer knows that demand is strong enough to permit an administered price that is sufficiently high to maintain profits in spite of some discouragement of demand.

Wartime Capacity Pressures

When the Wharton capacity index gets near 95 percent utilization and holds at that level for some time, we begin to see that significant price increases follow. This happened in connection with escalation of the war in Vietnam in 1965. In addition, wartime economic organization contains many inefficiencies. They generally result in rising costs and rising prices, with profit margins protected, at least to an extent.

Some International Aspects

Inflation can be explained and understood, to a great extent, in terms of a purely domestic or national discussion of issues and concepts. But modern inflation will never be fully understood or appreciated without specific reference to some international matters.

The food/fuel price rises of recent years have been largely international in origin, spread, and ultimate scope. They could have come about as purely domestic issues in terms of supply, cost, and capacity limits. In fact, the food shortages of 1972-73 originated in poor harvests in the U.S.S.R. and China. These giant consumers went to the world market and bid up prices that affected consumers in grain-producing countries (as well as elsewhere) and high food prices became a worldwide phenomenon. Additional commodity speculation in international foods and in various industrial materials led to worldwide price increases. Next, we had the oil embargo by Arab countries on exports to some oil-importing countries, followed by high world prices. These events resulted in worldwide transmission of inflationary shocks.

In these senses, cost inflation was international, but could have been domestic as well. However, there is something new in the world economy that makes inflation analysis a bit more elusive: the system of floating exchange rates. Floating rates are not new as far as world economic history is concerned, but they are new, on a broad scale, for the period that dates from the end of World War II. In the world of floating rates—managed floats, that is—we have seen some wide swings. The new set of rates that followed the Smithsonian agreement of December 1971 and the secondary wave of February/March 1973 gave rise to large-scale exchange rate appreciation in Germany and Japan and depreciation in the United States and elsewhere. At the beginning, Japanese prices could be restrained because the heavy purchases of raw materials were transacted at low yen costs as a result of the yen's becoming so valuable. The same was true of Germany. Eventually, high oil prices and high prices for other necessary commodities hit Japan so seriously that they were leaders in the world inflation race.

In the case of the United States, a good portion of the 1974 inflation rate has been attributed to exchange depreciation of the dollar. More serious cases of inflation transmittal occurred in 1976, in the United Kingdom and Italy. Speculation against the pound sterling and Italian lira forced the exchange rates down. This development moved both countries off their target paths for inflation control. They had been planning on reducing inflation rates, which exceeded 20 percent, to the single-digit range by 1976 or 1977. Both countries had rates of about 20 percent in 1976, and they are expected to stay firmly in two-digit range in 1977. France experienced the same pressures on trade account, franc valuation, and inflation in 1976, but to a much lesser extent.

British plans for dealing with inflation involved the implementation of an incomes policy—the so-called social contract—by which wages were restrained in order to hold price increases down. When workers saw prices rise far above target values, after the depreciation of sterling, they had second thoughts about renewing the social contract. The fact that speculation and exchange depreciation were responsible for much of the inflation meant very little to the workers; they saw prices eroding their purchasing power, and that was the telling fact. The workers have been temporarily persuaded to maintain the social contract, but international events could upset the delicate balance.

At present, the pound has regained strength and many economists are urging the Bank of England to let it rise in order to hold down inflation rates. Correspondingly, much of the argument for fiscal stimuli to be undertaken by Germany and Japan has been coupled with a plea for simultaneous currency appreciation. The fiscal policies have potential for generating inflation, and this could be offset by yen and Deutsch mark upward floats.

As more experience is gained with the system of floating rates, we shall understand more about the processes of their determination and the relationships to inflation rates. From what we have seen since 1971, it is clear that there are many inflationary aspects.

The Significance of Inflation

Some economists argue that inflation really doesn't matter because society can always adopt compensatory schemes to counteract the damage of inflation, implying that it presents a livable economic situation. I strongly deny this and argue that it is important for our society to face the inflation problem and deal with it head-on.

First, and most evident, inflation brings many inequities in economic life. Some groups profit, some are hurt, and some come out on neutral ground. It is in dealing with the inequities for fixed (nominal) income recipients, debtors, and creditors that some economists believe that they can compensate for the unjust social ills of inflation.

I would argue, however, that adjustments tend to be slow, there are lags in compensation, and some adjustments are not likely to be made. I think it is wrong to let a situation develop that calls for adjustment and then *hope* that full compensation can be implemented.

A second ill of inflation is its inefficiency. Apart from spending time making compensatory adjustments, people must pursue economically inefficient activities in trying to get ahead of inflation. They must seek out inflation-proof economic acquisitions for the sake of inflation protection, and not necessarily because these acquisitions are intrinsically desirable from an economic viewpoint. The cost overruns that have often occurred in major projects for military procurement under periods of military stress are indicative of what to expect in the way of inefficiency.

The most important aspect of inflation in making it a dangerous economic episode, however, is not generally recognized or pointed out as such. It is its instability. That is, the underlying economic dynamics may lead to explosive movements. Inflation in the aftermath of World War I brought economic dislocation and instability to the world in the form of one of mankind's worst calamities. Once inflation begins to accelerate, it may soon get out of hand and lead to economic breakdown. Unstable elements of mass psychology may develop. If we can avoid such a dangerous economic environment, we should do so at all costs, because otherwise we may be dragged into an economic no-man's-land.

Inflation and Economic Activity

The subtitle of this section should be, "Does inflation cause unemployment?" There is a point of view, forcefully expressed by Alan Greenspan and generally reflecting the views of the former United States administration, that inflation causes unemployment. The reasoning behind that view suggests that once inflation is recognized, the authorities—especially the monetary authorities but also the Treasury authorities—will start tightening the general policy lines. Tight credit conditions would slow down economic activity and lead to reduced output with higher unemployment. If this is the chain of reasoning, it should be pointed out that things need not work out this way. The authorities could respond differently and not adopt policies that are deliberately calculated to generate recession with unemployment.

My way of looking at the issues is quite different. I would say that there is no fixed relation between inflation and unemployment. It is incorrect to argue that there is a fixed and well-defined relation. From an empirical point of view, the relation between inflation and unemployment has been studied all over the world and the evidence is quite mixed. If any empirical generalization can be made, it is that there is no significant correlation between inflation and unemployment. Some countries have experienced fast growth with low rates of inflation, as well as high rates of inflation. In low-growth countries the same conclusion with respect to inflation obtains. It can go either way. If we were to construct a four-cell, 2 by 2 table,

Growth

	Low	High
Inflation High		
Low		

we would find no preponderant tendency for cross-economy operations to cluster in any particular pattern. The hypothesis that inflation causes unemployment would imply a positive correlation between the two variables.

If there is no empirical relation between inflation and unemployment, can we explain, in a structural sense, what underlying process is at work? Unemployment and inflation are endogenous variables in the larger economic system. Therefore, both can be explained by the exogenous variables that drive the economy. Essentially, we have two separate relationships:

$$\text{Unemployment} = f_u \text{ (exogenous factors)}$$
$$\text{Inflation} = f_i \text{ (exogenous factors)}$$

Any observed relation between inflation and unemployment must be brought about by the simultaneous movement of given exogenous factors in the two functions, f_u and f_i. It is all a matter of how exogenous forces are shaping the direction of the economy. I can suggest some kinds of exogenous shifts that induce a positive relation between unemployment and inflation and some kinds that induce an inverse relation between them. If we have an external disturbance such as occurred in 1973-75, whereby world food and fuel price changes brought inflation on a large scale to the United States, we would expect to find a positive association, leading to rising prices and rising unemployment. This was thought to be an anomaly when it occurred, but it is actually a natural outcome of the way external disturbances were affecting the internal economy.

On the other hand, if the exogenous factors were changing through a regular fiscal stimulus, either by raising public expenditures or by lowering domestic income taxes, we would find higher rates of activity, leading to lower unemployment and upward pressure on prices. This would be the now familiar tradeoff relation between inflation and unemployment, resulting in an inverse or negative relationship.

Actually, the main theoretical line of thought, running counter to the quantity theory of money, is the analysis built on the Phillips curve. In that analysis, there is an inverse relationship between wage change and unemployment. Wage changes, in turn, are positively related to prices; therefore an inverse tradeoff results between price change (inflation) and unemployment. It appears that the proponents of the theory that inflation causes unemployment are claiming that a positive correlation exists between inflation and unemployment. At the same time, they caution against policy measures to stimulate the economy, bringing down the rate of unemployment and generating wage increases that lead to price increases. They imply by this line of reasoning that there is an inverse relationship between inflation and unemployment, the tradeoff relation associated with Phillips curve analysis.

Are they asking to have it both ways—a positive relation between inflation and unemployment and a negative relation between inflation and unemployment? It is not unknown in economic analysis that more than one relation may simultaneously associate a pair or more of variables, but the burden of logical demonstration is on the "other side" to clarify exactly what is meant and the lines of reasoning that show that inflation causes unemployment at the same time that a tradeoff relation exists.

Policies to Deal with Inflation

There is widespread but not universal recognition of the evils and dangers of inflation. What might be done about it? The answers will depend on theoretical analysis of the underlying causes and explanation of inflation.

An inflation policy that has frequently come into the contemporary national debate is the technique of indexing. I would not call this an anti-inflation policy. It is more a technique for trying to live with inflation—more or less accepting it as inevitable. By "indexing" we generally mean the varying of wage rates, transfer payments, tax payments, interest payments, debt principal repayment, bank account asset valuation, etc., to changes in the general price index. Some countries have mandated indexing to cover wages, transfers, taxes and, occasionally, bank accounts and bonds. In some cases only selected items are indexed. The principal argument for indexing is equity and justice, to try to soften the inflationary blow as it strikes different people with varying force. For example, the very proper concern with the economic position of pensioners in an inflationary environment has led, in the United States, to the practical indexing of social security benefits to the consumer price index, although the benefit adjustments have usually lagged behind needs.

A virtue of indexing is that it may preserve the free-market calculus, but a corresponding deficiency is that more and more comprehensive indexing may destabilize the dynamics of the economy at large. The welfare gains from free-market economics are usually based on a static analysis that assumes equilibrium can be reached with relatively little effort. This analysis fails to take dynamic considerations into account.

Contemporary econometric research suggests the following conjecture: As an economic system is more and more fully indexed, it may become more and more vulnerable to external shocks that set up dynamic price movements. In a fully indexed system, the movements of prices swing in wider amplitudes than would be the case in an unindexed economy.

This conjecture was suggested by the following piece of research. An extended version of the Klein-Goldberger model was constructed for the United States, bringing data up to date through 1974. The system was simulated in two modes: one as is, in terms of best fit to the actual data of the economy, and one with as much indexing as possible. Disturbances are then superimposed in the equation system. It is observed that the amplitude of movement of the general price level is greater in the indexed than in the nonindexed case.

Inflation can be attacked through monetary policy,

usually following an assumption of validity for the quantity theory of money. The results are by now familiar. Strict monetary policy in the face of advancing inflation cuts down capital formation and consumer spending, often bringing recession. On two recent occasions, public authorities tried to slow down the economy and succeeded in both cases, 1969 and 1975, in engineering recessions. The latter recession was uncomfortably severe. We might characterize this approach as fighting inflation with higher unemployment. This is something that the new United States administration said it would not do.

What has been brought about through strict monetary policy can also be accomplished through strict fiscal policy, although the success of fiscal tightening does not depend on acceptance of the quantity theory of money.

An inelegant and blunt anti-inflation program can be mounted through the use of direct controls. Controls over prices and wages served the country well in the emergency situation of World War II, but hardly anyone wants to go through the reinstitution of a bureaucratic structure for price control and its implementation without the cohesive driving force of national determination to win a war. Some forms of wage and price control cannot be ruled out as a possible solution to contemporary inflation problems, but it is a last-resort policy, to be considered only after all else has failed.

Contrary to much popular belief and inherent cynical attitudes, an incomes policy does not imply wage and price controls. Controls over income flows, particularly if implemented on a macro level, are far different from detailed and direct wage and price control. The Kennedy guidelines, which seemed to work well until the airline machinists brought them down in 1966, did not involve the creation of a price police force such as we had during World War II. Other income policies can be designed in connection with taxing powers to achieve the desired results without resort to direct price controls. Many different proposals have been made. One idea is to tax employers who grant expansive wage increases, that is, above a stated guideline level. This is the Weintraub-Wallich proposal. Another scheme is to offer workers personal tax relief in return for wage restraint, again according to a numerical guideline. This is an Okun proposal and exists in a special form in the United Kingdom today.

My preference would be for a scheme tied to productivity growth. Specifically, the allowable percentage rates of increase in wage rates (macro) and in after-tax profits per unit of capital (macro) would be the same as the long-run productivity growth trend, measured as a historical moving average of productivity growth. This scheme would rely on industrywide collective bargaining by large unions to set the pattern for wage rates and on Treasury authorities to fix corporate taxes to set the pattern for after-tax profits. Since these would be macro guidelines, there would be ample scope for variation above and below national averages. The advantages of this approach are that it is a fair-shares policy and does not go to the extreme of direct price controls. In econometric model simulations, it produces very favorable outcomes, enabling the economy to grow rapidly without causing inflation.

To carry out incomes policy schemes there must be a national understanding in the form of a social compact negotiated between employer and employee groups. If the President were to take the initiative boldly, he might be able to negotiate such a compact. Once the economy reaches a full-employment growth path and holds at that position for some time, there is very likely to be a buildup of inflationary pressure, threatening the continued existence of full employment and full-capacity operation of the economy, unless backed by some sort of social compact.

In spite of some problems of logical consistency, noted previously in this presentation, there is wide acceptance of the notion that a tradeoff exists, forcing us as a nation to opt for stable prices or full employment, but not for both together. I regard this as a defeatist notion and would argue for policies that attempt to realize both together: full employment with price stability. In this respect, we should be looking for policies that improve the tradeoff.

Let me begin the citation of such policies by noting that the problem may get easier in the not-too-distant future. There is good reason to believe, on demographic grounds, that labor force growth may slow down after 1980. If this happens, our problem is most severe at an intermediate term level and may be more tractable in the 1980s.

The tradeoff point is likely to be reached substantially before we get to full employment—at some point between 5 and 6 percent unemployment. We could probably get to this position with conventional macro policies along monetary and fiscal lines. But to get to really full employment, without inflation, we need to turn to *structural* policies to deal with the long-term unemployed, the unemployed in groups that are discriminated against, the unemployed in young age groups, the unemployed in large urban centers. Structural policies may consist of:
  a. Fostering more competition,
  b. Job-training programs to improve the quality of human capital, and
  c. Large-scale investment in fixed capital that promises to contribute to productivity growth.

(a)   Some restrictive practices have grown up over the years that contribute to higher prices. They may have seemed reasonable on other grounds in the past, but now they are counterproductive in the fight against inflation.

Regulation of airline fares, regulation of bank interest payments, some restrictive labor practices, and some import restrictions all tend to make domestic prices higher than they would be if the restrictive practices were relaxed.

(b) Combined private and public sector job-training schemes that provide jobs with upward mobility to those in the labor force who show promise of receptivity to training should be initiated. It is thought that one million persons could be absorbed in such schemes. Sharing the effort between the private and the public sectors is designed to provide relief to the public budget in connection with such schemes. For them to be successful, they must be of sufficient duration to provide appropriate training and they must contribute to the production of goods for which there is an adequate market. This means that such programs must be set in the context of simultaneous demand-side programs for sustaining sales of full-employment output throughout the economy.

(c) As a nation, we have come through years of the affluent society with some expensive and wasteful habits (particularly with regard to energy use). For some years, we should now devote a slightly larger share of our GNP to fixed capital formation. This should serve to enhance productivity, and productivity gains are central to the fight against inflation. Larger investments in both human and fixed capital are essential to the improvement of productivity.

The joint attack on inflation and unemployment requires some imagination and the adoption of some unconventional economic policies. There is hope that improvement can be achieved simultaneously on both fronts if a sincere national effort is made.

Business and Government:
The Changing Relationship

Murray L. Weidenbaum*

A FUNDAMENTAL CHANGE is now taking place in business–government relations in the United States, a change so pervasive that it is tantamount to a second "managerial revolution." The current wave of government regulation of business is changing the locus of decision making and the responsibility for a large portion of private-sector activities.

The first managerial revolution was noted by Adolph A. Berle and Gardner C. Means more than four decades ago and given the title by James Burnham three decades ago. They were referring to the shift of decision-making power from the formal owners of the modern corporation to professional managers. In the view of Berle and Means, the "owner" of industrial wealth is left with a mere symbol of ownership, while the power and the substance are transferred to a separate group in whose hands lies the actual control.[1]

---

*The author is indebted to Linda Rockwood for many helpful suggestions and comments on an earlier draft. This paper draws on a variety of previous works, including Murray L. Weidenbaum, *Business, Government, and the Public* (Englewood Cliffs, N.J.: Prentice-Hall, 1977), and Murray L. Weidenbaum and Linda Rockwood, "Corporate Planning versus Government Planning," *Public Interest* (Winter 1977).

Now under way, the second shift in business decision making is from professional management, selected by the corporation itself, to the vast cadre of government planners and regulators who influence and often control the key managerial decisions of the typical business firm. This second managerial revolution is forcing a fundamental change in the nature of our society. The traditional concerns and debates in business-government relations (Are we moving toward socialism? Are we in the grips of a military-industrial complex?) should be recognized as dealing with an age that already has passed. There are few important examples of outright nationalization of industry in the United States; rather, the tendency is for government to take over, or at least share, many key aspects of decision making in all firms.[2]

The Changing Locus of Economic Decision Making

The change that our industrial economy is undergoing must be viewed as a bureaucratic phenomenon. In the main, it is not intentional, or even noticeable to the day-to-day observer. It involves the lawful efforts of governmental civil servants as they go about their routine and assigned activities, tasks which in concept are hard to criticize. Who is opposed to cleaning up the environment? Or enhancing job safety? Or improving consumer products? Or eliminating discrimination? Or promoting full employment?

Extending the analysis of Berle, Means, and Burnham to the current situation, we see that it is not who owns the means of production but who makes the key decisions that is crucial in determining the distribution of public and private power. If we step back and assess the long-term impacts on the private enterprise system that flow from the rapidly growing host of government inspections, regulations, reviews, and subsidies, we find that the entire business-government relationship is being changed in the process. To be sure, the process is far from complete, and it proceeds unevenly in its various phases. But the results to date are clear enough: the government, increasingly, is participating in and often controlling the kinds of decisions which are at the heart of the capitalistic system.

It is important to understand that this relatively silent bureaucratic revolution is not intended to undermine the capitalistic system. The men and women involved are patriotic citizens who are attempting to carry out high-priority national objectives which are considered to be basic to the quality of life in America.

Yet those who have assigned these tasks, the Congress and the Executive Branch leadership, have often failed to appreciate the significance of what they have been doing. If specific laws had been proposed or regulations promulgated for the government formally to take over private risk-bearing and initiative, the problem would have been faced head-on and the changes likely defeated. The most ambitious proposals to extend government influence over the private sector, such as the Full Employment and Balanced Growth Act (the Humphrey-Hawkins bill), refer to encouraging the "optimum contribution of the private sector" and to the desire to "foster and promote free competitive enterprise."

That, of course, is one of the most significant and difficult aspects of the development that we are analyzing. This silent managerial revolution is unintentional. It is merely an unexpected by-product—but far more than a minor side effect—of the expanding role of government in our modern society. Most proponents of greater government planning and regulation truly believe that this ambitious activity can be superimposed on the business system without damaging its central and desirable features, such as risk-taking, efficiency and productivity, scientific progress, and enhanced employment opportunities.

And the expansion of government involvement is self-reinforcing. When the government issues rules and regulations that reduce the ability of the private sector to provide productive employment, the pressures rise for government to serve as the employer of "last resort." Government policies, adding to the cost of private production, result in price increases which, in turn, can be a justification for greater governmental involvement in wage and price decisions. And when government policies sharply curtail the ability of the private sector to generate adequate savings to finance economic growth, not only is the government looked upon as the banker of last resort, but the basic vitality of the capitalistic system is called into question.

The New Wave of Government Regulation

It is hard to overestimate the rapid expansion of government involvement in business in the United States. The new type—and almost infinite variety—of governmental regulation of business is not limited to the traditional regulatory agencies, such as the Interstate Commerce Commission, the Civil Aeronautics Board, the Federal Communications Commission, and the Federal Power Commission. Rather, the line-operating departments and bureaus of government—the Departments of Agriculture, Commerce, Health-Education-Welfare, Interior, Justice, Labor, Transportation, and Treasury—are now involved in actions that affect virtually every firm.

Pressures for Regulation

Impetus for this expanded government participation is provided by a variety of consumer groups, environmental organizations, civil rights advocates, labor unions, and other citizens' institutions. In many cases, the increasing regulation reflects public and congressional concern that traditional federal and state-local programs have not been effective. The new wave of regulation is also reinforced by the belief that the private sector itself is responsible for many of the problems facing society: pollution, discrimination in employment, unsafe products, unhealthy working environments, misleading financial reporting, and so forth. The present trends in federal government regulation in the United States do not represent an abrupt departure from an idealized free-market economy but rather the rapid intensification of the long-term expansion of government influence over the private sector.

Government regulation at times can be justified as a logical response to imperfections in the private economy or what economists call "failures" in the normal market system. Examples of such situations are pollution of the environment, inadequate industrial safety practices, and long-term health hazards. Voluntary action to deal with such problems may place a firm under a competitive disadvantage. The specific company in attempting to correct the situation, would tend to bear the full costs, while the benefits of the improvement would be widely dispersed in the society. "Free riders," who do not make the expensive changes, may nevertheless share in the benefits (those "externalities").

An example of this situation is provided by the regulation of pollution in the motor vehicle industry. The basic justification for government's setting standards for automobiles—particularly in the pollution area, where so much of the benefit goes to society as a whole—was clearly stated by John J. Riccardo, president of Chrysler:

> A large part of the public will not voluntarily spend extra money to install emission control systems which

will help clean the air. Any manufacturer who installs and charges for such equipment while his competition doesn't soon finds he is losing sales and customers. In cases like this, a Government standard requiring everyone to have such equipment is the only way to protect both the public and the manufacturer.[3]

Range of Regulation

Certainly the majority of public policy changes affecting business-government relations in recent years has been in the direction of greater governmental involvement: environmental controls, job safety inspections, equal employment opportunity enforcement, consumer product safety regulations, energy restrictions, and recording and reporting of items varying from domestic illnesses to foreign currency transactions. Indeed, when we attempt to look at the emerging business-government relationship from the business executive's viewpoint, a very considerable public presence is evident in what ostensibly, or at least historically, have been private affairs.

No business official today, neither the head of a large company nor the corner grocer, can operate without considering a multitude of governmental restrictions and regulations. His or her costs and profits can be affected as much by a bill passed in Washington as by a management decision in the front office or a customer's decision at the checkout counter. The types of management decisions which increasingly are subject to governmental influence, review, or control are fundamental to the business system: What lines of business to go into? What products can be produced? Which investments can be financed? Under what conditions can products be produced? Where can they be made? How can they be marketed? What prices can be charged? What profit can be made?

Virtually every major department of the typical industrial corporation in the United States has one or more counterparts in a federal agency that controls or strongly influences its internal decision making. The scientists in corporate research laboratories now receive much of their guidance from lawyers in federal, state, and local regulatory agencies. The engineers in manufacturing departments must abide by standards promulgated by Labor Department authorities. Marketing divisions must follow procedures established by government administrators in product safety agencies. The location of facilities must be in conformance with a variety of environmental statutes. The activities of personnel staffs are increasingly restricted by the various executive agencies concerned with employment conditions. Finance departments often bear the brunt of the rising paperwork burden imposed on business by government agencies that seem to assume that information is a free good—or, in any event, that more is always better than less.

Many types of government controls accompany programs that are basically promotional in nature. For example, the federal government provides subsidies to ship builders and ship operators. However, to qualify for the government assistance, the ships must incorporate costly national defense and safety features, which unsubsidized vessels do without.

Government procurement contracts spell out not only what goods and services the contractors must provide but also how they should go about producing them. These requirements range from hiring and training minority groups, to adopting federally set wage and hour standards, to favoring depressed areas and small business firms in subcontracting.

The tax collector also serves as regulator or at least as a source of strong influence. Using the carrot of tax incentives, the federal government fosters greater social responsibility on the part of business. Internal Revenue Service provisions that have been adopted in recent years include tax credits for hiring certain categories of people (minority groups), tax deferrals for income from exports, and outright tax reductions for investing in capital goods (the investment tax credit). At times there is a direct linkage between taxes and controls. For example, to qualify for rapid tax amortization of pollution control devices, a company's facility must first be certified by both the state involved and the regional office of the Environmental Protection Agency. For company contributions to qualify as a tax deduction, a pension program must meet detailed requirements spelled out in the Employee Retirement Income Security Act of 1974.

Recent Additions

The current wave of government regulation is not merely an intensification of traditional activities; in good measure, it is a new departure and requires a new way of thinking. The standard theory of government regulation of business, which is still in general use and has dominated professional and public thinking on the subject, is based on the model of the Interstate Commerce Commission. Under this approach, a federal commission is established to regulate a specific industry, with the related concern of promoting the well-being of that industry. Often the public or consumer interest is viewed as subordinated, or even ignored, as the agency focuses on the needs and concerns of the industry it is regulating.

In some cases—because of the unique expertise possessed by the members of the industry or the industry's enticements for regulators who leave government employment—the regulatory commission may become a captive of the industry it is supposed to regulate. At least, this is a popularly held view of the development of the regulatory process. Actual practice of course varies by agency and jurisdiction and over time. In addition to the ICC, examples of this development, which have been cited from time to time, include the Civil Aeronautics Board, the Federal Communications Commission, the Federal Power Commission, and the Federal Maritime Commission.

A distinction may be made between the approaches of political scientists and economists, although the practical effects of their conclusions are quite similar. The "capture" theory is expressed in its most basic form in the work of political scientists who have examined the regulatory process.[4] Especially in recent years, economists have developed a more general theory of the regulatory process as the arena in which various interest groups invest their resources in order to affect an outcome more to their liking. The capture theory, in this view, is explained in terms of the dominance of a small group whose stake is relatively large over the entire society, whose interests are more diffused. The usual end result is the familiar one of the interests of the regulated industry prevailing over those of the consumer.[5]

Professor Louis Jaffe of the Harvard Law School has provided an interesting variation of the capture theme. In his view, whether a regulatory commission does or does not serve the ends of industry is much less important than whether it serves the correct ends. On reflection, those aims may or may not correspond to the desires of the industry that is regulated.[6] Moreover, Professor James Wilson cites important examples, such as the Federal Power Commission's controls over natural gas pricing, where the agency's actions are clearly adverse to the industry's well-being (and, in that case, the public's also).

Although the traditional type of federal regulation of business continues, the new regulatory efforts, established by Congress in recent years, follow a fundamentally different pattern. However, evaluating these newer regulatory efforts with the ICC model is inappropriate and can lead to undesirable public policy. The new federal regulatory agencies are, simultaneously, broader in the scope of their jurisdiction than the ICC-CAB-FCC-FPC model yet, in important aspects, far more restricted. This anomaly lies at the heart of the problem of relating their efforts to national interests (see figure 1).

In the cases of the Environmental Protection Agency, the Equal Employment Opportunity Commission, the Consumer Product Safety Commission, the Occupational Safety and Health Administration, and the Federal Energy Administration, the regulatory agency is not limited to a single industry. The jurisdiction of each of these relative newcomers to the federal bureaucracy extends to the bulk of the private sector and at times to productive activities in the public sector itself. It is this far-ranging characteristic that makes it impractical for any single industry to dominate these regulatory bodies and activities in the manner of the traditional model. What industry is going to capture the EEOC or OSHA? Or would have the incentive to do so?

Yet in comparison to the older agencies that are oriented to specific industries, in many important ways the newer federal regulators operate in a much smaller sphere. That is, they are not concerned with the totality of a company or industry but only with the limited segment of operations which falls under their jurisdiction. The ICC, for example, must pay attention to the basic mission of the trucking industry, to provide transportation services to the public, as part of its supervision of rates and entry into the trucking business. The EPA, on the other hand, is interested almost exclusively in the effect

VARIATIONS IN FEDERAL REGULATION OF BUSINESS

Category of Industry or Sector of the Economy

Regulatory Agency	Railroads and Trucking	Airlines	Radio and TV	Utilities	Manufacturing				Interest Group
					Drugs	Autos	Defense Products		
Consumer Product Safety Commission								→	Consumer Groups
Occupational Safety and Health Administration								→	Labor Unions
Equal Employment Opportunity Commission								→	Civil Rights Groups
Environmental Protection Agency								→	Ecologists
	ICC →	CAB →	FCC →	FPC →	FDA →	Traffic Safety Administration →	Renegotiation Board →		

of trucking operations on the environment. This restriction prevents the EPA from developing a close concern with the overall well-being of any company or industry. Rather, it can result in a total lack of concern for the effects of its actions on a company or industry.

If there is any special interest that may come to dominate such a functionally oriented agency, it is one that is preoccupied with its specific task: ecologists, unions, civil rights groups, and consumerists. Thus little if any attention may be given to the basic mission of the industry to provide goods and services to the public. Also ignored are cross-cutting concerns or matters that are broader than the charter of the regulating agency, such as productivity, economic growth, employment, cost to the consumer, effects on overall living standards, and inflationary impacts. While the traditional regulatory agencies may be said to be overly concerned at times with economic growth and productive efficiency, the newer programs move to a different beat. Their impetus comes from such social considerations as improving the quality of life, both on and off the job, and changing the distribution of income among the various groups in the society.

To be sure, there are important cases which combine or blend the old and the new forms of regulation. The Securities and Exchange Commission is a good example. In one aspect of its activities, it regulates a specific branch of the economy, the securities industry; yet many of its rules also influence the way in which a great many companies prepare their financial statements and reports to shareholders. Nor are economywide regulatory agencies a recent creation; the Federal Trade Commission has existed for six decades. Moreover, a few one-industry agencies continue to be created, notably the Commodity Futures Trading Commission, which regulates the financial markets that deal with products of agriculture and other extractive industries.

The result of the new approach to government regulation of business is the reverse of the traditional situation. Rather than being dominated by a given industry, the new type of federal regulatory activity is far more likely to utilize the resources of various industries, or to ignore their needs, in order to further the specific objectives of the agency and those of its special-interest constituency. The traditional theory of regulation is geared to a world where the regulators—as well as the various adversaries in the process—are concerned with prices and entry. But the new breed of regulators—and certainly the so-called public-interest groups that support their efforts—are usually oblivious to the effects of their actions on prices and entry (or exit). In fact, many of them condemn as "cold hearted," "callous," or worse any consideration of cost or other economic factors in deliberations on product, personnel, or environmental safety. The following statement by a member of the Consumer Product Safety Commission is representative of the views of the regulators in the new type of agencies:

> "Any time consumer safety is threatened, we're going to go for the company's throat. . . . When it involves a product that is unsafe, I don't care how much it costs the company to correct the problem."[7]

Strange and varying alliances arise in promoting a given type of regulatory activity—or in pushing for reform. The business firms and labor unions in a regulated industry often become strong supporters of the traditional industry-oriented commission which they have learned to live with, if not to dominate. They may join ranks to oppose efforts by consumer groups and economists to cut back on the extent of the "protective" regulation. This has been most apparent in the railroad and trucking industries.

In contrast, consumer groups advocate expanding the new types of cross-cutting or functional regulation. In this effort, they often are joined by labor groups, particularly in the occupational health area, where reform efforts may be led by coalitions of business groups and economists who are concerned with excessive costs and other consequences of the specialized regulatory activities. These alliances may shift from time to time. Specific safety regulations for automobiles may be opposed by unions and companies in the motor vehicle industry, although the two groups may differ strongly on job safety standards. Labor, management, and local governments may present a united opposition against environmental efforts which are viewed as hurting the economies of their community,[8] although some of these groups may advocate general ecological advances. The older consumer organizations may become more concerned with the ultimate cost to the consumer of expanding governmental activities than the newer and more militant groups that emphasize public control over private-sector activities.

Some Perspective

Perspective is needed. Although in general the scope of federal influence is expanding, there are limits to this trend. Some controls do end. For example, in January 1974 the federal government terminated the interest equalization tax on American holdings of foreign stocks and bonds and the five-year-old program of controls over direct investments abroad by United States corporations. Simultaneously, the Federal Reserve System ended its guidelines for limiting lending and investments overseas by United States banks and other financial institutions.

The general wage and price control system was allowed to expire at the end of April 1974. Restraints on price increases since then have been limited to energy and to regulated industries that operate under federal authorizations, such as the airlines and the railroads.

Also, the federal government does not adopt every suggestion for increasing government regulation of the private sector. In April 1974 the Food and Drug Administration rejected a petition by thirty-seven congressmen and nine consumer groups calling for warning labels on all packaged foods that do not list each ingredient. The FDA commissioner stated that the proposed label would confuse and mislead consumers, and expressed doubt whether most buyers read the relatively simple statement of ingredients that is now available.

The Consumer Product Safety Commission rejected the petition of Ralph Nader's Health Research Group, which warned of the "imminent hazard to the public health" represented by lead-wick candles. The petition asserted that small children might chew or swallow the candles, taking lead into their system, and candle-lit suppers would result in "meals literally bathed in lead." In a letter to the Nader Group, Commissioner Laurence M. Kushner stated that the petition "was drawn either with abysmal ignorance of elementary physical science, colossal intent to deceive the public or both. The calculations, in the petition, of possible concentrations of lead in air which might result from burning such candles were based on assumptions that are physically impossible."[9]

Although the precise changes that will occur in the years ahead are a matter for conjecture, the overall trend seems to be fairly clear: on balance, there is likely to be more, not less, government intervention in internal business decision making. Despite differences in philosophy and outlook, changes in control of the Executive Branch and in the composition of Congress and the judiciary seem to have little effect in altering that trend.

Government regulation, however, is a phenomenon that

is still in the process of development, rather than having attained a "steady state." The basic factors that cause the changes are diverse, ranging from concern by some with the quality of life to the desire by others to increase the social responsiveness of business enterprise. Yet virtually all proposals for changes in public policy that affect business are variations on a single predictable theme: to increase the scope and degree of governmental involvement while shifting costs from the federal purse to the products and services that consumers buy.

No balanced evaluation of the overall practice of government regulation really fits the notion of benign and wise officials who always make sensible decisions in society's greater interests. Numerous adverse side effects and other costs are evident, as well as substantial benefits to society.

When we examine the sector of industry that is most subject to government supervision—defense production—the results are disconcerting. It is precisely the companies that are most heavily dependent on military contracts that report the largest cost overruns and the greatest delays. The society does not get the benefit of efficiency and innovation expected from private industry. The ultimate consequences of governmental assumption of basic entrepreneurial and managerial functions are surely worthy of considerable attention and study.

The Costs of Government Involvement

Even though most of the changes in government control or influence on business decision making are designed to benefit the public, a neglected aspect is increasingly apparent as the widening array of regulations takes its full effect: it is the consumer who ultimately pays the added costs that so often result. This is especially true in the newer regulatory programs which are the particular concern of this study: the functional or cross-industry types of social legislation. In the more traditional areas, many regulations deal with natural monopolies, such as utilities. In some of these one-industry regulatory efforts, however, government actions may be anticompetitive and thus ultimately costly to the consumer. Interstate trucking furnishes a cogent example, where federal regulation is in large degree a barrier to entry, protecting existing firms against possible new entrants.

Impacts on Cost of Production

There are many ways in which government regulation can increase the cost of production and thus the prices that consumers pay. Productivity is often adversely affected by the variety of regulations that are designed to improve the quality of the work environment. To the extent that the regulations reduce accidents and absenteeism, they contribute positively to output and thus to economic welfare. But in practice this is not often the result, as the emphasis is on essentially "bureaucratic" concerns. Forms are filled out. Safety rules are posted. Inspections are made. Fines are levied. But no significant reduction in industrial accident rates results.

In the job safety program, as in numerous other areas of government involvement, the original concern of the public and the Congress has been converted to the practice of not violating the rules and regulations. "You won't get into trouble if you don't violate the safety standards" is the response, even if as many accidents occur as before. The emphasis shifts to such trivia as raising and answering these types of questions: How big is a hole? When is a roof a floor? How frequently must spittoons be cleaned? The results, in terms of the safety objective, are almost invariably disappointing. Yet the reaction is virtually predictable: redouble the effort—more forms, more inspections—and thus higher costs to the taxpayer and higher prices to the consumer.

Examples of obvious inefficiencies or trivia in regulation of business are not hard to come by. Capable, intelligent and well-meaning administrators, delegating decisions to capable, intelligent and well-meaning subordinates, cannot specify in advance all of the correct or desirable exceptions to general rules. Upon examination, reported examples of regulatory nonsense seldom turn out to be mere flukes. They are almost an inevitable result of the rapid expansion of the scope and variety of regulatory functions in the United States in recent years.

Federal regulation has other costs to the economy. Increases in product prices which result from meeting more stringent government regulations have an added impact on the inflation rate to the extent that they trigger further increases in product costs due to automatic escalator clauses in wage and other agreements (which provide for wages and other items to rise automatically with increases in general price indexes).

Impacts on Capital Formation

In addition, regulation affects the prospects for economic growth and productivity by levying a claim for a rising share of new capital formation. This is most evident in the environmental and safety areas. Examination of the flow of capital spending by American manufacturing companies just prior to the recent recession is revealing. In 1969 the total new investment in plant and equipment in the entire manufacturing sector of the American economy came to $26 billion. The annual totals rose in the following years. But when the effect of inflation is eliminated, it can be seen that four years later, in 1973, total capital spending by United States manufacturing companies was no higher. In "real terms," it was approximately $26 billion in both years.

That is not the end of the story, however. In 1973 a much larger proportion of capital outlays was devoted to meeting government regulatory requirements in the pollution and safety areas—$3 billion more. Hence, although the economy and its needs had been growing substantially in those four years, the real annual investment in modernization and new capital had actually been declining. The situation was worsened by the accelerated rate at which existing manufacturing facilities were being closed down, due in part to the rapidly rising costs of meeting government regulations. About 350 foundries in the United States were closed down during 1971-74 because they could not meet requirements such as those imposed by the Environmental Protection Agency and the Occupational Safety and Health Administration. This may help explain why the American economy, for a substantial part of 1973, appeared to lack needed productive capacity, despite what had been large nominal annual investments in new plant and equipment in preceding years.

The governmental decision-making process can have other adverse effects on capital formation by introducing uncertainty about the future of regulations governing the introduction of new processes and products. An example is furnished in a November 1975 report of a task force of the President's Energy Resources Council dealing with the possibility of developing a new synthetic fuel industry. In evaluating the impact of the Federal Water Pollution Control Act amendments of 1972, the task force reported: "It would be next to impossible at this time to predict the impact of these requirements on synthetic fuels production."[10]

With reference to the National Environmental Policy Act of 1969, the task force stated that the major uncertainty was not whether a project would be allowed to proceed but rather the length of time it would be delayed pending the issuance of an environmental impact statement that would stand up in court. The task force pointed out: "The cost of such delays (construction, financing and inflated raw materials and labor costs) is an obvious potential hazard to any synfuels project."

Impacts on Employment

Government regulation, albeit unintentionally, can have strongly adverse effects on employment. This has been demonstrated in the minimum-wage area where teenagers have increasingly been priced out of labor markets. A recent study has shown that the 1966 increase in the statutory minimum wage resulted by 1972, in teenage employment in the United States being 320,000 lower than it otherwise would have been. As a result of that one increase in the compulsory minimum wage, the youth unemployment rate in 1972 was 3.8 percent higher than otherwise would have been the case.[11]

In construction labor—where unemployment rates are substantially above the national average—government regulation also acts to price a segment of the work force out of competitive labor markets. Under the Davis-Bacon legislation, the Secretary of Labor promulgates "prevailing" wages to be paid on federal and federally supported construction projects. A variety of studies has shown that these federally mandated wage rates are often above those that actually prevail in the labor market where the work is to be done.[12]

Although to a minor degree, the equal employment opportunity program may tend to increase unemployment by delaying the filling of job vacancies. To the extent that employers must undergo protracted job searches prior to hiring employees, the average length of unemployment is likely to be longer. It is not uncommon for a position to remain unfilled, despite the availability of an adequate labor supply at market prices, because the governmental regulatory requirements for advertising have not been met.

Impacts on Innovation

The price that the nation may be paying for the expansion of governmental power is the attenuation of the risk-bearing and entrepreneurial characteristics of the private enterprise system, which, at least in the past, have contributed so effectively to rapid rates of innovation, productivity, growth, and progress. One of the hidden costs of federal regulation is the reduced rate of innovation as the result of governmental restrictions. The longer it takes for some change to be approved by a federal regulatory agency—a new or improved product, a more efficient production process, etc.—the less likely it is that the change will be made.

As William D. Carey of the American Association for the Advancement of Science has stated, "Government may imagine that it is neutral toward the rate and quality of technological risk-taking, but it is not . . . regulatory policies aimed at the public interest rarely consider impacts on innovation."[13] The adverse effect of regulation on innovation is likely to be felt more strongly by smaller firms and thus to have an anticompetitive impact. According to Dr. Mitchell Zavon, president of the American Association of Poison Control Centers,

> We've got to the point in regulatory action where its become so costly and risky to bring out products

that only the very largest firms can afford to engage in these risky ventures. To bring out a new pesticide you have to figure a cost of $7,000,000 and seven years of time.[14]

To the extent that management attention is diverted from traditional product development, production, and marketing concerns to meeting governmentally imposed social requirements, a significant but subtle bureaucratization of corporate activity may result. In the employee pension area, for example, the recently enacted pension regulation has shifted much of the concern of the pension fund management from maximizing the return on the contributions to following a more cautious approach of minimizing the likelihood that the fund managers will be criticized for their investment decisions. It thus becomes safer—although not necessarily more desirable to the covered employees—for the pension managers to keep more detailed records of their deliberations, to hire more outside experts (so that the responsibility can be diluted), and to avoid innovative investments.

State and Local Regulation

The maze of government regulations is intensified when when one considers the laws administered by state and local governments. In addition to regulating many of the same areas as the federal government, such as pollution control and job safety, state and local governments introduce numerous other types of regulation. Some of these regulations also can have anticompetitive impacts.

The requirement for licensing certain professions is a popular means of limiting the number of those engaged in a certain trade. Every state has at least ten licensing boards and some have as many as forty. Occupations that require licenses range from television repair to midwifery.

New Hampshire licenses lightning-rod salesmen, and Hawaii tattoo artists. A majority of states have laws forbidding the advertising of prices of prescription drugs, eyeglasses, or hearing aids. As a result, in Texas, where price advertising is allowed, single-vision eyeglasses sell for $20; in California, which has a price blackout, the same glasses can cost $60.[15] Thirty-six states have "fair trade" laws which require retailers to charge the prices set by the manufacturer. These laws prevent price competition and insure dealers an attractive markup on the merchandise.

A cogent example of a sector that is experiencing duplication of regulation by federal, state, and local agencies is the milk industry. Sixty-one federal milk "orders" and eighteen state laws fix the prices that processors must pay dairy farmers. Some states go a step further and fix resale prices, in addition to producer prices. These regulatory programs set prices that producers must pay for approximately 90 percent of the fluid milk and milk products consumed in the United States.

Milk plants also experience an extraordinary variety of inspections by more than 20,000 state, county, local, and municipal milk jurisdictions in the United States. A USDA study reveals that milk plants are inspected about twenty-four times annually, even though the Public Health Service recommends only two a year. In one state, milk plants averaged ninety-five inspections during a year. One milk plant, licensed by 250 local governments, three states, and twenty other agencies reported that it was inspected forty-seven times in one month in 1964.[16]

The Power of Regulators

The foolishness and uneconomical effects that can flow from government regulation pale when they are compared to the arbitrary power that can be exerted by the personnel of the regulatory agencies. Many liberals are outraged by the arbitrary "no knock" powers of federal investigative agencies, yet they readily ignore the unchallenged "no knock" power used by federal agencies in their regulation of private business.

The Supreme Court has ruled that air pollution inspectors do not need search warrants to enter the property of suspected polluters, as long as they do not enter areas that are closed to the public. Unannounced inspections, which were conducted without warrants, were held not to be in violation of constitutional protections against unreasonable search and seizure. The inspectors of the Labor Department's Occupational Safety and Health Administration (OSHA) can go further. They have no-knock power to enter the premises of virtually any business in the United States, without a warrant or even prior announcement, to inspect for health and safety violations. Jail terms are provided in the OSHA law for anyone tipping off a "raid."

The awesome power exercised by government regulators is often unappreciated by the public, as well as by the regulators themselves, and the ban on spray adhesives is worthy of attention. On the surface, it appears to have been, at most, only a matter of excessive caution on the part of the Consumer Product Safety Commission. On August 20, 1973, the commission banned certain brands of aerosol spray adhesives as an imminent hazard. Its decision was based primarily on the preliminary findings of one academic researcher who claimed that they could cause birth defects. After careful research failed to corroborate the initial report, the commission lifted the ban, on March 1, 1974.

Why do I mention this case? Depriving consumers of spray adhesives for less than seven months does not seem too harsh in view of the desire to avoid serious threats to people's health. In fact, the admission of error on the part of the commission is commendable; its prompt recision of the initial action would seem to break speed records for a government agency. But there is more to the story.

According to a survey performed by researchers at the New York State Department of Health and the Albany Medical College, at least nine pregnant women who had used the spray adhesives reacted to the news of the commission's initial decision by undergoing abortions for fear of producing babies with birth defects.[17] They could not reverse their decision when the regulatory commission reversed its. The episode illustrates some of the unexpected and unnecessary consequences that can arise from the false identification of an environmental agent as a mutagen or teratogen. The sadness of this case is hardly reduced by the fact that everyone involved was trying to promote the public health and safety. Indeed, this case illustrates the dilemma of government regulators: had the commission failed to ban spray adhesives and the initial research been validated, an equally sad scenario could have resulted.

In any event, the spray-adhesive experience should give pause to those who oppose any analytical examination of government regulation in the health and safety area with the refrain, "How can you measure the value of a human life?" The point is that it is not always accurate to presume that a government safety regulation, costly or not, necessarily saves human lives.

Another recent case of government regulation adversely affecting human health relates to the Consumer Product Safety Commission's 1972 ruling requiring manufacturers of children's sleepwear to meet a designated flammability standard. In 1977 the commission banned all garments made with one of the major fire-resistant chemicals, after learning that there is more likelihood that the children would get cancer from the chemical than that they would be injured by the clothing's catching fire.[18] It is unlikely that the companies that were required to replace the pajamas that they had produced to meet the commission's original standards will be reimbursed for the large losses resulting from the commission's changing its mind.

Feedback Effects on Business Decision Making

The power of government regulators also can give rise to a feedback effect on private decision making—and some of these feedbacks can be extremely negative from public and private viewpoints. In part, the highly publicized illegal gifts by business corporations may have been a response to this phenomenon. Frankly, this assertion will take a bit of explaining to avoid being misunderstood.

Business has been taking it on the chin as revelations of so-called political slush funds have been uncovered. Although it is altogether fitting that lawbreaking be exposed and punished, and corporate contributions to federal election campaigns are illegal, an aspect of illegal business contributions to political causes has been ignored. When we turn to more traditional types of crime, we find that progressive thinking is not limited to punishment but extends to uncovering the causes. By identifying the conditions that breed crime, it is hoped that public policy can be modified so as to reduce or eliminate those conditions—a preventive approach to lawbreaking.

A parallel can be drawn to the Watergate-related cases of unlawful corporate political contributions and their attempted coverup. What was the underlying force for these illegal acts? The dominant motive was not usually a desire to enrich the individual corporate executives who were involved, or even to enhance their positions in the company. Neither was the typical motive the desire to get the federal government to grant a particular favor to the firm ("favors" in the form of government contracts were the object of many payments to citizens of other nations). Rather, the illegal contributions were usually a response, often reluctant, to requests from the political representatives of a powerful governmental administration which was in the position to do great harm to the company. Whether the government would abuse its vast power in the absence of an adequate payment was a risk that many corporate managements decided not to take.

It is not surprising that so many of the executives who were implicated held positions in corporations that are dependent upon government in important ways—for defense contracts in the case of large manufacturing companies, for government-approved route structures in the case of airlines, and for special subsidies in the case of natural resource industries. It may not be too wide of the mark to consider many of those illegal corporate payments a form of "protection money" to prevent action harmful to the company. Viewed in this light, the underlying cause of this type of white-collar crime does not arise within the company itself. Rather, the fundamental reason for such lawbreaking is the tremendous and arbitrary power that the society has given the federal government over the private sector.

Thus eradication of this form of white-collar crime involves more than tighter auditing standards and improved laws on political financing, although such changes are surely necessary. It also requires restraint in further expansion of governmental power over the private sector. From this point of view, it would be helpful to reduce the arbitrary decision-making authority that many federal agencies now possess in their dealings with business firms.

My basic point should not be misunderstood, and it bears repetition. Lawbreaking, whether by business executives or others, should not be condoned. It should be ferreted out and punished according to law. Simultaneously, it is naive—and ineffective as well—to ignore the basic forces that give rise to the lawbreaking. In business contributions to the political process, much of the basic thrust comes from the awesome power that, through the political process, government has been given over business, power that ranges from awarding contracts and subsidies to withholding approval of new products and facilities. The situation is not improved to the extent that election finance reforms, whether intentional or not, tend to enhance the political position of labor over business. Most of labor's political efforts do not show up in the official reports and hence are not subject to comparable legal limitations.

Obvious examples include the virtual full-time assignment of union organizers and clerks to get-out-the-vote duty. In 1976, more than 10 million calls were placed from the telephone banks of the AFL-CIO's Committee on Political Education (COPE). Approximately 180,000 "volunteers" were involved in its car pools and doorbell ringing. As nonprofit organizations, labor unions pay low, subsidized rates on their mailings, including campaign material.[19] According to Al Barkan, the director of COPE, "As important as funding is in politics, however, COPE's strength is people, always most of all people—the thousands of volunteers who make the COPE program go and who provide the nuts-and-bolts support services that are so crucial to winning elections. . . ."[20]

It seems that a double standard is operating with reference to these unreported items. What companies or trade associations would dare assign their executives to full-time campaigning as part of their paid work? What companies would devote their reports to shareholders and executives to the blatant campaigning in which unions engage with impunity? Of course, there is nothing illegal in those union activities. However, the national environment is such that companies are afraid to engage in similar types of lawful activity for fear of an outburst of enraged media and citizen reaction. The unfortunate result, as we have seen in some cases, is to encourage business executives to utilize illegal subterfuges to attempt to redress the political balance. Personally, I would prohibit both unions and companies from engaging in these activities. Certainly, the status quo is unfair, and it is unrealistic to ignore its motivating role in the illegal and immoral activities of business, which we all condemn.

Centralized Planning: Another Wave of Government Intervention?

In a very real sense, the current national debate on the role of government power and regulation is taking place on two very distinct levels. On one level, there is growing interest in applying benefit–cost analysis to regulation, in giving Congress veto power over individual regulations, and in other procedural changes. Simultaneously, an effort is under way which, in effect, would leapfrog this entire generation of regulatory activity.

The second approach is in terms of a more basic expansion in government influence on private-sector decision making by means of establishing a formal system of national economic planning. In recent years, the Federal Budget and the annual *Economic Report of the President* have been utilized as vehicles for presenting broad-gauge, long-term projections of economic conditions and national priorities, at least to the extent that the changing allocation of federal financial resources indicates revisions in the relative importance of the major program and policy areas.

Increasing attention is being given to specific proposals such as the Humphrey-Javits and Humphrey-Hawkins bills, which would augment and focus the power of the federal government in an attempt to achieve a major reduction in unemployment and to attain other important national objectives. One of the stock arguments used by the proponents of these bills is that if private industry does long-range planning, why can't the government do the same? The short answer is that the national government's doing the planning for the American people would not be the same as individual private organization's doing their own planning.

There are fundamental differences between business planning and government planning. Boiled down to fundamentals, we are dealing with the difference between forecasting and reacting to the future, on the one hand, and trying to control it, on the other. Corporate planning of necessity is based on attempting to persuade society that it ought to purchase the goods or services produced by that firm. The controls that may accompany the plan are internally oriented. In striking contrast, the government is sovereign; its planning ultimately involves coercion, the use of its power to achieve the results it desires. Its controls are thus externally oriented, extending over the entire society.

The proponents of a formal national economic planning system say that they would not set specific goals for General Motors, General Electric, General Foods, or any other individual firm. But what would they do if these companies would not conduct themselves, in the aggregate, in accord with the national plan? Would they leave the actual results to chance or to the free market?

Hardly. The Initiative Committee for National Economic Planning states that the planning office "would try to induce the relevant industries to act accordingly."[21] And the inducements are not trivial. The government's powers to tax, to purchase, to subsidize, to "assist," and to regulate are awesome. Even the most powerful planning system in the private sector lacks the ability to levy taxes.

Much of the rhetoric in favor of a centralized economic planning system is in terms of merely developing better information; but even a cursory examination of the literature on American business planning demonstrates that planning is intended to be far more than improved information accumulation. A standard definition is: "A plan is a predetermined course of action . . . to accomplish a specific set of . . . objectives."[22] One expert offers the most terse rendition: "Planning is to a large extent the job of making things happen that would not otherwise occur."[23] Nor do the proponents of centralized government planning leave the matter in any doubt. They clearly state: "The heart of planning is to go from information to action."[24]

The essence of the difference between public and private planning is the locus of decision making. If Ford or General Motors or Chrysler are not selling as many automobiles as they had planned, there are a limited number of things they can do about it. They can, within their available resources, lower prices or change the nature of the product. But—as is evidenced by the demise of the Edsel, the LaSalle, and the DeSoto—they may be forced to abandon the project. The consumer remains the ultimate decision maker.

The situation is far different in the public sector. If the government does not believe that the American public is buying enough cars, it can lower the price as much as it likes through tax reductions. Also, it can subsidize the private manufacture of automobiles or simply take over the the ownership of the industry.

My point is not that private planning does not involve control but that those who are subject to its control powers are very different. Once a private corporation adopts its long-range plan, it may push the various units of the corporation to meet their goals and objectives. But the controls are internal: incentives and sanctions, focusing on the officers and employees of the corporation. If things go wrong, the onus falls on them. Government planning, in contrast, concentrates on "guiding" or "influencing"—and thus ultimately controlling—the activities of the entire nation. If things go wrong in public-sector planning, it is the taxpayer and consumer who bear the burden.

Two types of government planning need to be distinguished. The external planning, which is discussed here, involves all sorts of extensions of government powers over the private sector. A second type of government planning is more internally oriented and is comparable to private-sector planning. It relates to the management of government's own activities. In advocating national planning, Senator Hubert Humphrey deals with this second aspect:

> The manner in which we are presently utilizing government resources and government agencies is a haphazard, helter-skelter enterprise . . . we can show that with some planning in our government, just a modest amount, a little more than we're doing, we can reduce government costs and get better governmental services.[25]

Perhaps a government that is conducted on such a haphazard, helter-skelter basis should not be given the extremely ambitious task of managing the entire economy prior to getting its own house in order.

A comprehensive scheme of national economic planning could shift the focus of private enterprise even further away from dealing with market forces and meeting consumer demands and even closer to reaching an accomodation with an ever more powerful governmental bureaucracy. The payoff from traditional consumer market research might be less than from new efforts to persuade the government to adopt more generous production targets for an industry.

We could readily conjure up visions of civilian companies following some of the practices of that branch of American industry, defense production, which is now most closely tied to governmental decision making. Business-financed hunting lodges and fishing trips for civilian government planners might seem merely to follow a defense industry tradition. Such public-sector "marketing" activities would be a low-priority use of business resources. Yet, given the incentive of any organization to try to prosper in the environment it faces, this result would not be surprising under a system of strong national economic planning.

The advocates of centralized planning who base their case on an extension of business planning activities also overestimate the state of the art in the private sector. No amount of formalized planning has eliminated any company's uncertainty about future technological change, the vagaries of weather, discoveries of energy or other natural resources, outbreaks of war, assassinations of national leaders, or even shifts in the desires of the fickle consumer. Even if one discounts the shortcomings of existing business planning techniques, the differences between business and government decision making are fundamental.

Business planning is based on the traditional assumption that the ultimate decisions on the allocation of resources in the society are to be made by individual consumers. Government planning is predicated on a fundamentally different set of assumptions. Government determines what it considers to be in the society's overall interests. If the public does not respond accordingly, it is not the planners who are considered to be at fault. Rather, new and more effective devices are developed to get the public to accommodate to the planners' view of the good (or great) society. The greatest danger of adopting centralized planning is that it will, perhaps unintentionally at first but inevitably as its initial results prove disappointing, propel our country toward greater government control over individual behavior. Serious disadvantages are no guarantee, of course, against the enactment of some form of centralized planning in the years ahead.

Reforming the Regulatory Process

Numerous bills have been introduced in Congress to reform one or more aspects of the process of governmental regulation of business activities. Some would "deregulate" specific industries, notably railroads and airlines, by dismantling a portion or all of the control apparatus established by the old-line regulatory commissions. Other approaches are in terms of compulsory periodic review of each major regulatory program ("sunset" bills), designed to determine whether reform is worthwhile in the light of changing circumstances. Most of these bills do not provide objective criteria to guide the presidential and congressional reviews which would be required under the proposed statutes.

Benefit-Cost Analysis

Many economists favor another route, which essentially is complementary and not competitive with the legalistic approaches. It is to urge that benefit-cost calculations be required in the governmental regulatory process as a means of correcting the various shortcomings that were described earlier.

Specific proposals have been made to limit the promulgation of new regulations to instances where it can be demonstrated that the benefits to society will exceed the imposed costs. A greater emphasis on economic rationality surely is commendable, even after necessary allowances are made for the limitations of the state of the art of benefit-cost estimation. The proponents of regulatory programs often tend to oppose any of these changes in the belief that they would weaken the programs. The measures that may be adopted are likely to be marginal. Some intermediate position is, at best, the most realistic outcome: continuation of existing federal regulatory activities, although their administration may involve providing more economic justification.

But beyond questions of mathematical measurement of the gains and losses from government intervention, there is a strong case for considering the overall scope of government regulation. As Professor Daniel Bell contends, the central question is not the efficacy of any particular agency or specific issue of regulation, but the regulatory process itself and its consequences for the corporation and for the society.[26]

A new way of looking at the microeconomic effects of government programs is needed, and a parallel can be drawn to macroeconomic policymaking, where important and at times conflicting objectives are recognized. Attempts at reconciliation or tradeoff are made, as among economic growth, employment, income distribution, and price stability. At the programmatic or microeconomic level, it is also necessary to reconcile the goals of specific government programs with other important national objectives, which are not now the concern of many of those agencies. In part, this reconciliation needs to be made at the most basic stages of the governmental process—when the President proposes and the Congress enacts a new regulatory program. In developing an environmental statute, for example, it should be kept in mind that a cleaner environment is not the only important need of the society, and that each increment of regulatory power reduces the extent of individual freedom and private-sector discretion. At the operating level, legislators, together with the administrators of the statute, need to understand that there may be more than one way of achieving the desired objective, and that the search for efficient solutions is not synonomous with a "green eyeshade" approach to social goals.

Some type of quantitative analysis, such as benefit–cost estimation, may have a useful role in that reconciliation process. But policy formation needs to proceed beyond another set of so-called economic impact statements. First of all, the costs and the benefits of government actions need to be more than examined; they should be weighed one against the other. In the process, the actual or proposed regulations that generate excessive costs should be modified or eliminated. But we need to go beyond the direct impact on price and include the relationship to productivity, capital formation, and innovation. This decentralized approach to government policy would involve the setting of analytical and measurement standards for government regulatory agencies by a unit that is not involved in conducting regulatory programs, such as the General Accounting Office or the Office of Management and Budget. This arms' length relationship is needed to assure uniformity in the measurement of benefits, costs, and other effects. Such standards would reduce the temptation of individual regulatory agencies to present self-serving justifications of their existing activities, albeit in a new economic framework.

Much would depend on the "teeth" that would be put into any required economic impact statement. Merely legislating the performance of some economic analysis by an unsympathetic regulator would delay the regulatory process and thus make it more costly. But limiting government regulation to instances where the total benefits to society exceed the costs would be a major departure. It could significantly slow down, if not reverse, the rising trend of federal regulation of business.

To an economist, government regulation should be carried to the point where the incremental benefits equal the incremental costs, and no further. (Indeed, this is the basic criterion which is generally used to screen proposed government investments in physical resources.) Overregulation—which can be defined as situations where the costs exceed the benefits—should be avoided. But if policymakers tend to ignore or downplay the costs, we are bound to operate in the zone of overregulation, which is likely where we are today. In cases where the benefits cannot be quantified in dollar terms, the approach could be a search for the least costly means of achieving the regulatory objectives. The literature on cost-effectiveness analysis can be drawn upon for that purpose.[27]

Critics of benefit-cost analysis often tend to emphasize the importance of the distribution of the benefits and the costs, rather than their relative size. Although this is surely an important point, empirical results may often be different from those they anticipate. Rather than the benefits being widely dispersed in the society and the costs borne by a few (supposedly the wealthy), the reverse may often be the case. Highly skilled (and therefore well-remunerated) union members may benefit from more stringent job safety standards and the consuming public may pay for them in the form of higher product prices.

The debate over relatively cheap (for example, ear protectors) versus relatively expensive engineering approaches (for example, $263,000 per worker in the textile industry) to noisy work environments is very instructive.[28] OSHA and the unions have advocated the more expensive approach. If the workers had their choice, many of them might prefer receiving a $100,000 bonus, and wearing earplugs, to the costly reengineering of the workplace. The present regulatory arrangements do not permit such choice; the market tends to, albeit imperfectly.

The Range of Costs and Effects

In making judgments on which regulations to adopt, the governmental decision-making body should pay particular attention to several overhead areas that are often neglected: the monitoring costs to the government, the information costs imposed on both the public and private sectors, and the related private costs of compliance and/or avoidance. It is hardly coincidental that, simultaneous with the recent expansion of governmental regulatory activity, the cost of legal departments and legal services has been one of the most rapidly growing segments of company budgets. In a different connection, Daniel Patrick Moynihan stated:

> As government tries to do more, it will find it accomplishes less. That amounts to the discovery that administrative ability is not a free good, and in the absence of it the best intentioned programs can turn out to be calamities.[29]

It is important to build into the governmental processes those incentives which would encourage government officials to give greater weight to the costs and other sideeffects that are generated by the actions they take. Limiting new regulations to instances where it can be demonstrated that net benefits accrue to society as a whole is one such device. At the operational level, attention should be given to use of the budget process as an added tool of management of regulation. In cases where an agency's regulations generate more costs than benefits, its budget for the coming year should be reduced, and vice versa. Another possibility for making the regulatory agencies more sensitive to the cost they impose on the society is for Congress to give them "budgets" of private costs that they can cause to be incurred by their regulations. Thus not only would an agency be given a budget of X million dollars for operating costs, but also Y billion dollars of social costs that they can incur during the year. In justifying their budget requests for those "social costs," the agencies would also be required to estimate the offsetting social benefits.[30]

Wide dissemination of the data on the economic impacts of government regulation might serve to alter the balance of interest-group forces that are exerting pressures on the decision-making process. At the present time, it often appears that the interest groups which would benefit from a regulation are well aware of these benefits and thus mobilize their forces in favor of greater regulation.

Attitudes toward Regulation

More basically, however, attitudes need to be changed. Experience under the job safety program provides a striking point, for although the government's safety rules, regulations, and requirements have resulted in billions of dollars in public and private outlays, the goal of a safer work environment has not been achieved.

A more satisfying answer requires a fundamental change in approach to regulation, and one that is not limited to the job safety program (which is used here merely as an illustration). If the objective of public policy is, say, to reduce accidents, it should focus directly on the reduction of accidents. Excessively detailed regulations often are merely a substitute for hard policy decisions. Rather than issuing citations to employers who fail to fill out the forms correctly or who do not post the correct notices, the punitive actions ought to be aimed at those with the worst safety records. (Variable insurance rates may perform a similar function.) As the accident rates decline toward some sensible average standard, the fines could be reduced or eliminated.

The government should not be concerned with how a company achieves the objective of a safer working environment. Some may find it more efficient to change work rules, others to buy new equipment, and still others to retrain workers. That is precisely the kind of business-management task that government should avoid, but which now dominates so many of these regulatory programs. Without diminishing the responsibility of employers, the federal occupational safety and health law should extend its sanctions to employees, especially those whose negligence endangers other employees. The purpose is not to be harsh but to set effective incentives to achieve society's objectives. This can be a preferred alternative to government's specifying the details of what it considers to be "acceptable" private action.

A recent case in point is the proposed job safety standards for exposure to lead in the workplace. OSHA would require smelters, battery manufacturers, and other firms to install engineering controls that reduce the maximum exposure level from 200 micrograms of lead per cubic meter of air to 100 micrograms. The U.S. Council on Wage and Price Stability has estimated that meeting the proposed standards could cost the industries affected, and ultimately consumers, over $300 million a year. The council urges that OSHA allow each company to use the most efficient way of meeting the new standard, whether that requires costly engineering controls or some other method.[31]

Intensive employee training might be one of those alternative methods, if a study in the United Kingdom can serve as a guide. According to a report in the *British Journal of Industrial Medicine,* the lead exposures of employees in almost identical jobs differed by ratios of up to 4 to 1. This was attributed totally to personal differences in working habits.[32]

With reference to consumer protection regulation, an information strategy may often provide a sensible alternative. For the many visible hazards to which consumers voluntarily subject themselves, perhaps the most important consideration of public policy is to improve the individual's understanding of the risks that he or she is being subjected to. The kitchen knife may be the most prosaic example of such a visible hazard, which most individuals choose *not* to be protected from. Many pedestrians, likewise, voluntarily race across a busy intersection rather than wait for the traffic light to change.

Any realistic appraisal must acknowledge that important and positive benefits have resulted from many of the government's regulatory activities—in terms of less pollution, fewer product hazards, ending job discrimination, and other socially desirable objectives of our society. It should also be realized that these federal programs were established by Congress in response to a surge of rising public expectations about corporate performance.

But the "externalities" generated by federal regulation need not justify government's attempting to regulate every facet of private behavior. Indeed, the experience with governmental efforts indicates that further expansion of involvement in the detail of business decision making is likely to be self-defeating. Rather, restraint might yield great rewards. Also, alternatives to regulation need to be considered in adopting or improving public policy toward business. In the environmental area, for example, selective taxes on certain forms of pollution may be a more effective and economical means of achieving a given level of water quality than the promulgation of regulatory standards. In industry-type regulation, such as transportation, greater reliance on competition may be a more effective way of protecting the public interest. We need to acknowledge that many business executives, consciously or unconsciously, are adding to the probability of more government control over the economy by seeking ways to reduce competition. To illustrate this point, C. Jackson Grayson has cited letters that were sent to him by various businessmen when he was chairman of the U.S. Price Commission:

> We need government protection because we can't compete against the big companies.
>
> We must have minimum milk prices if we are to have an orderly market.
>
> If we allow liquor prices to fluctuate freely, competition will be ruinous and the Mafia might move in.[33]

Utilizing a variety of approaches to achieving the changes in business performance desired by public policy could help to attain another important objective. The continued expansion of regulatory activities inevitably gives rise to a question that is difficult to answer: Who will regulate the regulators?

One obvious response is to suggest a general consolidation into a few—or even one—comprehensive agency which would provide a built-in mechanism for reconciling conflicting regulatory activities. But, on reflection, such concentration of governmental power may be cause for even greater concern. Thus dispersal of government power over a variety of regulatory, tax, and other activities—as well as greater reliance on private market forces—may be a promising alternative response to the accountability question.

Many analysts tend to think of government legislative and

regulatory action as the only alternative to the market mechanism for solving the problem of external costs. Roger Noll has pointed out that the civil liability system also deals with this problem and that an extensive body of civil law defines and enforces various individual rights. Unfortunately, the civil liability system tends not to work very well when individual damages are small or difficult to measure, or when liability is difficult to ascertain.[34]

A Broader Viewpoint

By and large, the existing relationships between business and government in the United States can be described as basically adversary. In this view—which surely corresponds at least in part to the complex reality—government probes, inspects, taxes, influences, regulates, and punishes.

A striking contrast is sometimes drawn between this situation and what is often taken to be the dominant European and Japanese approach: a "partnership," or at least close cooperation, between business and government. The comparison has lead to suggestions that we import the foreign model of business–government relations. It is often contended that such closer working relations would improve our competitive position abroad as well as enhance productivity at home. However, this approach could have fundamental shortcomings, resulting in submerging the public, and especially the consumer, interest in economic matters.

Therefore, yet another approach may be more appropriate for the United States: the eclectic combination of greater dependence on the competitive business system with streamlined government regulation to deal with private actions which do not sufficiently respond to market forces in meeting society's needs.

The relationships between the government of a society and the members of that society are delicate, involving careful balancing of many important considerations. Clearly, the polar alternative of complete freedom is unrealistic. Anarchy is hardly a sensible response to the needs of a modern, high-technology society. Society needs to use the powers of government to help its individual members achieve objectives that they cannot attain on their own. It is generally acknowledged that government needs to set the basic rules for enforcing contracts, to provide for the national defense, and to deal with environmental and other "external" effects of individual behavior.

Yet, as we look around the world, it is apparent that it is all too easy to move substantially beyond that position to the undesirable situation where the state directs the details of the day-to-day lives of the individual members of that society. This is that other polar alternative, the totalitarian state.

It is pertinent that such a strong advocate of the free market as Professor Hayek has made a compelling case for some significant government role in the economy, pointing out that he does not mean "that government should never concern itself with any economic matters." Rather, he says:

> A functioning market economy presupposes certain activities on the part of the state; there are some other such activities by which its functioning will be assisted; and it can tolerate many more, provided that they are of the kind which are compatible with a functioning market. . . . The range and principle, reconcilable with a free system is thus considerable.[35]

NOTES

1. A. A. Berle Jr. and G. C. Means, *The Modern Corporation and Private Property* (New York: Macmillan, 1932), p. 68. See also James Burnham, *The Managerial Revolution* (Bloomington, Ind.: Indiana University Press, 1941).
2. For details, see Murray L. Weidenbaum, *Government-Mandated Price Increases* (Washington: American Enterprise Institute for Public Policy Research, 1975).
3. John J. Riccardo, "Regulation: A Threat to Prosperity," *New York Times,* July 20, 1975, pp. 5, 12.
4. See Marver Bernstein, *Regulating Business by Independent Commission* (Princeton: Princeton University Press, 1955).
5. See George J. Stigler and Claire Friedland, "What Can Regulators Regulate? The Case of Electricity," *Journal of Law and Economics* (1962), no. 1; George J. Stigler, "The Theory of Economic Regulation," *Bell Journal of Economics and Management Science* (Autumn 1971); Richard A. Posner, "Theories of Economic Regulation," *Bell Journal of Economics and Management Science* (Autumn 1974).
6. See James Q. Wilson, "The Dead Hand of Regulation," *Public Interest* (Fall 1972), p. 41.
7. Cited in Gerald R. Rosen, "We're Going for Companies' Throats," *Dun's Review* (January 1973), pp. 36, 38.
8. Les Ledbetter, "Unions and Employers Fight Redwood Cutting Halt," *New York Times,* April 7, 1977, p. A18.
9. "Please Don't Eat the Candles," *Wall Street Journal,* January 16, 1974, p. 12.
10. Synfuels Interagency Task Force, *Recommendations for a Synthetic Fuels Commercialization Program,* Report submitted to the President's Energy Resources Council (Washington: Government Printing Office, 1975), 1:C-22.
11. James F. Ragan, Jr., *Minimum Wage Legislation and the Youth Labor Market,* Working Paper no. 8 (St. Louis: Washington University, 1976), Center for the Study of American Business, p. 29.
12. John P. Gould, *Davis-Bacon Act* (Washington: American Enterprise Institute for Public Policy Research, 1971); Armand J. Thieblot, Jr., *The Davis-Bacon Act* (Philadelphia: University of Pennsylvania, The Wharton School, 1975).
13. William D. Carey, "Muddling Through: Government and Technology," *Science,* April 4, 1975, p. 13.
14. Quoted in Sheila Rule, "Pesticide Regulations Called Too Stringent," *St. Louis Post-Dispatch,* September 18, 1974, p. 18F.
15. Lee Benham and Alexandra Benham, *Regulating through the Professions: A Perspective on Information Control* (St. Louis: Wash-

ington University, Center for the Study of American Business, July 1976), Publication no. 11.

16. Milk Industry Foundation, *Milk Facts, 1974* (Washington, 1974), p. 7; U.S. Food and Drug Administration, *A Study of State and Local Food and Drug Programs* (Washington, May 1965).

17. Comptroller General of the United States, *Banning of Two Toys and Certain Aerosol Spray Adhesives*, MWD-75-65 (Washington: U.S. General Accounting Office, 1975), pp. 13-30; Ernest B. Hook and Kristine Healy, "Consequences of a Nationwide Ban on Spray Adhesives Alleged to Be Human Teratogens and Mutagens," *Science*, February 13, 1976, pp. 566-567.

18. Marlene Cimons, "Massive Recall of Kids' Clothing," *St. Louis Globe-Democrat*, April 8, 1977, p. 1A.

19. A. H. Raskin, "COPE's Impact on Election Outcome," *New York Times*, December 28, 1976, p. 39.

20. Al Barkan, "U.S. Workers Have a Long Political History," *Viewpoint* (1st Quarter, 1976), p. 11.

21. "For a National Economic Planning System," *Challenge* (March/April 1976), pp. 52-53.

22. Malcolm H. Sherwood, Jr., "The Definition of Planning," in Robert J. Mockler, ed., *Readings in Business Planning and Policy Formulation* (New York: Appleton-Century-Crofts, 1972), p. 103.

23. David Ewing, *Long-Range Planning for Management* (New York: Harper & Row, 1964), p. 3.

24. "For a National Economic Planning System," *Challenge* (March/April 1975), p. 52.

25. "Planning Economic Policy, an Interview With Hubert H. Humphrey," *Challenge* (March/April 1975), p. 23.

26. Daniel Bell, "Too Much, Too Late: Reactions to Changing Social Values," in Neil Jacoby, ed., *The Business-Government Relationship* (Pacific Palisades: Goodyear Publishing Co., 1975), p. 19.

27. See Roland N. McKean, *Efficiency in Government through Systems Analysis* (New York: Wiley, 1958); Charles J. Hitch and Roland N. McKean, *The Economics of Defense in the Nuclear Age* (Cambridge, Mass.: Harvard University Press, 1960).

28. John F. Morrall III, *OSHA and U.S. Industry* (forthcoming).

29. Daniel Patrick Moynihan, "The Future of Federalism," in U.S. Advisory Commission on Intergovernmental Relations, *American Federalism* (Washington: Government Printing Office, 1975), p. 99.

30. The author is indebted to Charles Holt of the Urban Institute for this suggestion.

31. U.S. Council on Wage and Price Stability, *Council Comments on OSHA's Proposed Standard on Lead* (Washington: The Council, March 15, 1977).

32. M. K. Williams, E. King, and Joan Walford, "An Investigation of Lead Absorption in an Electric Accumulator Factory with the Use of

Personal Samples;" *British Journal of Industrial Medicine* (1969), no. 26, pp. 202-216.

33. C. Jackson Grayson, Jr., "Let's Get Back to the Competitive Market System," *Harvard Business Review* (November/December 1973), p. 104.

34. Roger Noll, *The Rationale for Mandated Cost Increases* (forthcoming).

35. F. A. Hayek, *The Constitution of Liberty* (Chicago: University of Chicago Press, 1960), pp. 222, 231.

The Social Control of Economic Power

Willard F. Mueller

FOR NEARLY nine decades, antitrust policy has been our chief instrument of social control of private economic power outside the "natural" monopoly industries. I begin my comments with my conclusion: Antitrust policy has failed in the past and will likely fail in the future. True, things might have been worse had it not been for the antitrust laws; but this is little consolation. To persist in relying solely on policies that have failed is to give substance to critics' assertions that antitrust is a charade, an anachronism, an excuse for inaction, an apology for the status quo.

What, then, must we do to be saved? Must we abandon the field to powerful private holders of economic power? Must we embrace a comprehensive system of controls, mandating that the holders of power perform in the public interest? Or must we nationalize much of our economic system to ensure that it performs as "the people" wish?

I find each of these alternatives unpalatable. Nor are they likely to be embraced by the American people in this century. Rather, I'm inclined toward an eclectic approach that continues policies that have worked, improves on those that show promise, and pursues new initiatives in areas where old ways have failed us.

But before we suggest any agenda for the social control of economic power, let us consider briefly the sources, magnitude, and consequences of excessive economic power.

The Power of the Modern Corporation

The economic power of the large modern corporation eclipses that of business enterprise that was familiar to the framers of the Sherman Act of 1890. Although the great merger movement around 1900 centralized control over much of manufacturing, at the time it was a much smaller part of the economy. Whereas in 1900 income originating in manufacturing and agriculture was about equal, today manufacturing is ten times larger. And relative to today's industrial giants, the "big" businesses around the turn of the century were as infants compared to adults. Today our two largest industrial corporations alone have greater sales (after adjusting for inflation) than did all manufacturing companies combined in 1900.

Moreover, the largest corporations have rather steadily expanded their share of an ever growing economy. Two hundred corporations control about two-thirds of all assets of corporations engaged primarily in manufacturing. Much of the expansion in the relative growth of the largest corporations was accomplished through mergers and acquisitions, especially during the merger movement of the 1920s and during the post-World War II movement that climaxed in 1966-69, but it continues today.

The typical large corporation is not simply big in absolute terms. It inhabits many industries, most of which are highly concentrated, and considers the world its marketplace. Although the pursuit of profit is still its major goal, this pursuit often takes the modern corporation into political affairs, both nationally and internationally.

In sum, the power of the large corporation is rooted in concentrated markets, in its conglomerate and multinational makeup, and in its huge size. These characteristics permit the large conglomerate corporation to engage in strategies that are not open to smaller firms.[1] Among these strategies are cross-subsidization and business reciprocity.

Cross-subsidization involves the use of resources from one line of business to expand, if necessary at a loss, another product line. Relatively specialized firms have limited opportunities and capacity to engage in cross-subsidization because their resources come from a single line of business. Conglomerate firms, on the other hand, operate in many product lines, in some of which they generally enjoy excess profits. They thus have both the opportunity and the capacity to engage in the practice.

Business reciprocity is the practice of buying from those who can buy from you. It becomes a potentially harmful competitive strategy when some firms in a market can make more sales on this basis than others. A single-line corporation has relatively few opportunities to pursue the practice, whereas a conglomerate firm that buys and sells a large variety and volume of products has the best opportunity to engage in reciprocal dealing.

Experience with reciprocal selling shows that it may be used successfully in a wide variety of market structures.[2] It adversely affects competition because it bypasses and distorts the competitive process. The result may be to increase the market position of reciprocity practitioners, raise entry barriers to would-be entrants, and discourage price rivalry when many market transactions are based on reciprocal agreements.

As conglomeration becomes increasingly commonplace

and the market is bypassed in large parts of the economy, "trade relations between the giant conglomerates tend to close a business circle. Left out are the firms with narrow product lines; as patterns of trade and trading partners emerge between particular groups of companies, entry by newcomers becomes more difficult."[3] The result, says *Fortune*, is that "the U.S. economy might end up completely dominated by conglomerates happily trading with each other in a new kind of cartel system."[4]

Reciprocal selling is a symptom of a larger problem involving the exchange of commercial favors among huge conglomerates that meet one another as competitors or are in buyer–seller relationships in many markets. Such multimarket contacts among conglomerates force them to recognize that their behavior in one market may have repercussions elsewhere. The result is that they tend to behave interdependently in many otherwise unrelated markets. We shall call this phenomenon conglomerate mutual interdependence and forbearance among actual and potential competitors. The result of such actions can affect market shares, entry, and pricing practices.

Although generally ignored by economists preoccupied with oligopoly problems, there are many examples of this phenomenon.[5] Even the *Wall Street Journal* recognized the problem when, at the height of merger activity in the late 1960s, it editorialized: "When ties among large corporations get too widespread and too involved, it seems to us they will impede the free movement of prices and capital even if the merged corporations are not in the same fields. Certainly the consolidation of various corporations into conglomerates could invite a vastly increased concentration of power, which gives us pause on both economic and social grounds."[6]

The national and international omnipresence of the huge corporation may best be visualized by an example.

My favorite for this purpose is ITT, which I have come to know better than most.[7] Like many other conglomerates, ITT is a leading defense and space company. But unlike most others, it is also a vast international organization which, according to its annual report, "is constantly at work around the clock—in 67 nations on six continents," in activities extending "from the Arctic to the Antarctic and quite literally from the bottom of the sea to the moon. . . ."

In 1961, ITT embarked on a major diversification-through-merger program. During 1961–68 it acquired fifty-two domestic and fifty-five foreign corporations, with the acquired domestic companies alone holding combined assets of about $1.5 billion. Duirng 1969 ITT's board of directors approved twenty-two domestic and eleven foreign acquisitions. The three largest—Hartford Fire Insurance Company, Grinnell Corporation, and Canteen Corporation—added over $2 billion, which brought its acquisitions total for the decade to near $4 billion, far ahead of any other company. Since 1969 it has acquired over fifty domestic and foreign firms.

Before engaging in this massive merger program in 1960, ITT ranked thirty-fourth among America's manufacturing companies and forty-third among the industrial companies of the world. In 1975 it ranked eleventh among America's industrial companies and, with 376,000 employees, was the fourth largest private industrial employer of the world.

ITT has retained its telecommunications leadership, ranking as the world's second largest manufacturer of such products and the largest outside the United States. Most of its other operations originated in acquisitions of leading firms in such diverse businesses as industrial and consumer electrical, electronic and other industrial products, life insurance, consumer finance, car rentals, hotels, baking, chemical cellulose and lumber, residential construction, and silica for the glass, chemical, metallurgical, ceramic and building industries.

If another merger of major dimensions, with American Broadcasting Company, had not been abandoned in January 1968, after a challenge by the Department of Justice, ITT would have been established also as a leader in U.S. radio and television broadcasting. It also would have been engaged in the operation of motion picture theaters, amusement centers, the manufacture and sale of phonograph records, and publishing.

Significantly, most of ITT's acquired assets came not from small, ailing companies but from profitable corporations that were already leaders in their field. Rayonier Corporation had assets of $292 million and was the world's leading producer of chemical cellulose. Continental Baking Company had assets of $186 million and was the world's largest baking and cake company. Avis, Inc., had assets of $49 million and was the world's second largest car rental system. Sheraton Corporation of America, with assets of $286 million, was the world's largest hotel and motel system. Levitt & Sons, Inc., with assets of $91 million, was the leading builder of single-family dwellings. Grinnell Corporation, with assets of $184 million, was the largest producer of automatic fire protection systems. Canteen Corporation had assets of $140 million and operated one of the largest vending machine systems. Hartford Fire Insurance Corporation was one of the oldest and largest property and casualty insurance writers, with assets of $1.9 billion.

Although ITT is primarily a manufacturing corporation, selling to and buying from thousands of other businesses, it also directly touches the lives of millions of consumers who can buy furnishings for their homes with personal loans from one of ITT's finance subsidiaries; buy radios, phonographs, tape recorders, and TV sets made by ITT in Germany and England; insure their homes at ITT-Hartford Fire Insurance; buy their life insurance from one of ITT's life insurance subsidiaries; invest their savings in ITT-Hamilton Management mutual funds; munch on ITT-Continental bakery products; savor an ITT-Smithfield ham; stay at hotels or motels owned by ITT-Sheraton; buy books from ITT's Bobbs-Merrill publishing division; or attend one of ITT's technical and business schools. Finally, had the ABC-ITT merger not been blocked by the Justice Department, Americans could have been ITT's guest for an evening of TV viewing.

Moreover, part of each of your tax dollar spent on defense and space programs goes to ITT, which is one of the nation's leading prime defense contractors. ITT maintains Washington's "hot line" to Moscow and mans the Air Force Distant Early Warning (DEW) system and the giant Ballistic Missile Early Warning System (BMEWS) sites in Greenland and Alaska.

With its numerous foreign operations, ITT is an important force in international economic affairs. Some ITT employees are better known in circles of international diplomacy than in business. They have included such notables as former U.N. Secretary General Trygve Lie as a director of ITT-Norway, former Belgium Premier Paul-Henry Spaak as a director of ITT-Belgium, two members of the British House of Lords, a member of the French National Assembly, and, at home, John A. McCone, former director of the CIA, and Eugene R. Black, a prominent figure in international economic and political circles. It is not unfair to ask whether such men have been on ITT's boards because of their business acumen or their prestige in international politics.

The growing multinational character of huge conglomerates raises important issues concerning their national allegiances. Their multinational makeup inevitably creates dual loyalties that make it difficult to perceive how their dealings at home and abroad serve the American national interest. This problem is well illustrated by ITT's involvement in the internal affairs of Chile and elsewhere.[8]

Quite clearly, massive conglomerate corporations like ITT have dimensions of economic and political power extending beyond that held by the traditional large corporations which, while large in absolute terms, are more narrowly specialized in relatively few lines of industry.

An Agenda for Reform

There is no single, simple policy for dealing with excessive corporate power, domestically or internationally. I stress the word *excessive* lest the reader infer I believe our entire economic system is so infested with market power as to make any treatment an act in futility. All industries are not highly concentrated. Indeed, most industries are still quite competitive, and those that are not *could* be made more competitive if we had the desire and will to make them so. ITT is not the typical multinational corporation; nor do all holders of great power corrupt our political process.

Simply put, the market is not dead; nor are all large corporations peopled by mischievous evildoers, indifferent to the public interest. We must acknowledge, however, the reality that we have become heavily dependent upon large corporations for running our economy. Whether we like it or not, we must agree with ITT Chairman Harold Geneen's view that "increasingly, the larger corporations have become the primary custodians of making our entire system work." But acknowledging this reality also raises questions of legitimacy: Are the holders of power wielding it in the public interest, and if not, what can and should be done about it?

One of the chief problems in social reform is that too many citizens believe that because reform has failed in the past, it is doomed to fail in the future. They have become cynical and feel politically impotent, believing that noting can be done to ensure that the holders of power can be required to work in harmony with the broader public interest. Perhaps they are right. But we will never know unless they are provided with alternatives upon which they can express their views. What I propose is a modest beginning. If Americans can accomplish some of these reforms, an adequate constituency exists to accomplish other needed steps not mentioned here. Time permits covering only three areas:

Improving the effectiveness of antitrust;
The role of competition policy in incomes policy; and
Regulating the multinational corporation.

New Antitrust Initiatives

The antitrust laws are potentially powerful instruments for ensuring the maintenance or achievement of an effectively competitive economy. And they have had some outstanding victories in recent decades, most notably in controlling illegal mergers. The Sherman Act of 1890 and the Clayton Act of 1914 prohibited certain types of mergers, but subsequent Supreme Court decisions rendered them virtually meaningless policy instruments. This changed with the passage of the Celler-Kefauver Act of 1950. During the first twenty-five years of the act the antitrust agencies challenged over 1,000 acquisitions in over 400 complaints.[9] This effort has not involved an assault largely on small companies, as some have claimed. Practically all challenged acquisitions (measured by assets) involved large acquiring companies.[10] Indeed, most industrial corporations with assets exceeding $1 billion have been challenged one or more times.

Even more important than the actual relief resulting from these numerous challenges has been the deterrent effect of the resulting rules of law on other corporations contemplating mergers.[11] Enforcement has not, however, been an unqualified success. The belated assault on conglomerate mergers in 1969 foundered on what Henry Simons called "the orderly process of democratic corruption." The complaints, challenging three large mergers by ITT, were aborted by an ignominious consent settlement that prevented the Supreme Court from spelling out the rules of law in this important area.[12]

Since then, the antitrust agencies have become even more timid. They have shied away from challenging conglomerate mergers, as well as assumed a weaker stance toward other types of mergers.[13]

While the antitrust authorities have earned at least a "B" in their enforcement of the merger law, they deserve a failing grade in dealing with existing market power. Not only have they failed to attack the citadels of entrenched market power, but they have seldom even unlimbered their heavy artillery. And on the infrequent occasions when they venture into battle, their gunners soon grow weary and ultimately abandon the field, after signing a peace treaty that leaves the boundaries of power virtually unchanged.

Though economists may quibble about the precise degree and the trends of market power, few will deny that in many industries concentration already is too high and will not be eroded without public action. Virtually nothing has been done to make these industries more competitive. Fewer big Sherman Act monopoly cases have been initiated and brought to a successful conclusion in the last two decades than in the first two decades of the century. This despite the fact that contemporary antitrusters have many more resources than during Theodore Roosevelt's day, when the Antitrust Division "sallied out against the combined might of great corporations with a staff of five lawyers and four stenographers."[14]

Something, clearly, is amiss. It is not merely a matter of will, although since Thurmond Arnold's day few antitrust officials deserve citation in that thin book, "Profiles in Courage in the Pursuit of Competition."

Perhaps even more important than the absence of the will to act is the virtual impossibility of antitrusters' waging a successful legal battle with today's industrial giants. In recent years, the antitrust agencies have brought four big monopoly (or shared-monopoly) cases. The FTC brought shared-monopoly cases against the leading breakfast cereal corporations and eight leading petroleum companies. After more than four years, these cases are hopelessly bogged down in the early stages of legal proceedings. Nor has the Department of Justice fared better in its eight-year-old case against IBM and its three-year-old suit against AT&T. Both are far from resolution.

The chief problem is that the participants in these legal battles are so unevenly matched. The public often views government as a big, omnipotent force—and it certainly is when pitted against the lone citizen or the small business. But this is a false image when it comes to antitrust litigation. For example, AT&T is committed to spend $60 million defending itself, which is three times the total annual budget of the Antitrust Division. Let there be no mistake about it: the Antitrust Division is no match for "Mother Bell."

New approaches are required if antitrust is to be more than "an occasional legal ceremony," as Thurmond Arnold put it, perpetuating the myth that we actually have effective public policies to maintain competition. I have three

modest proposals to make antitrust a more viable force:
(1) the antitrust laws should be amended to simplify the
industrial restructuring process; (2) the legislative route
should be used to bring about selective restructuring; and
(3) the Federal Trade Commission should change its ways
and pursue the mission originally assigned it by Congress
in 1914.

Strengthening the Antitrust Laws

New legislation would accomplish more than merely
strengthening the Sherman Act. By debating the issues
and enacting new legislation, Congress and the President
would give the antitrust agencies a new mandate, reaffirming a vigorous procompetition policy through judicious industrial restructuring.

Two new antitrust laws are needed. One would involve
the general approach embraced by the late Senator Philip
Hart's proposed industrial reorganization act. The "act"
articulated standards for the *possession* of market power,
in contrast to existing case law that is preoccupied with
issues of competitive *intent* and *abuse* of market power.[15]
It provided for a "rebuttable presumption that monopoly
power is possessed" if certain structural and performance
criteria were met. This approach would greatly simplify
the legal standards, thereby enabling the Antitrust Division
to act more effectively and expeditiously.

There is also need for a new antimerger law. There is
mounting evidence that conglomerate mergers not only
adversely affect the competitive process in many subtle
ways, difficult to reach under existing laws; they also are
unnecessarily and irrevocably contributing to an enormous
centralization of economic resources in a few hands. Americans have long recognized that the centralization of economic

power is inimical to our political institutions as well as to our economy. Former Justice William O. Douglas articulated well the reasons why such unnecessary centralization should not be tolerated:

> Power that controls the economy should be in the hands of elected representatives of the people, not in the hands of an industrial oligarchy. Industrial power should be decentralized. It should be scattered into many hands so that the fortunes of the people will not be dependent on the whim or caprice, the political prejudices, the emotional stability of a few self-appointed men. The fact that they are not vicious men but respectable and social-minded is irrelevant.[16]

Because growing industrial conglomeration poses threats that transcend economists' narrow view of a merger's impact on individual markets, a higher standard should be used in judging *large* conglomerate mergers. Such legislation could require that before a large conglomerate merger is permitted, the Federal Trade Commission make an affirmative finding that (1) the merger did not have the effect of substantially lessening competition under existing law *and* (2) the merger is in the public interest because it promises to increase competition, efficiency, or provide other positive economic benefits *in which the public would share.* A large conglomerate merger might be defined as one where the acquiring firm has assets exceeding $250 million and the acquired assets exceed $50 million. The FTC would also be required to hold a public hearing at which the Department of Justice and third parties could present evidence on the likely effects of such mergers. Such a law would establish special standards for very large mergers and require antitrust authorities to account publicly for their decisions to *permit* or *reject* such mergers.

Legislatively Mandated Industrial Restructuring

Even with a new antitrust law, the antitrust agencies will still be ill equipped to tackle certain big tasks. In these cases, history proves the advantages of direct legislative action to bring about industrial restructuring. Although not used for over three decades, this approach has accomplished much more restructuring than has the Sherman Act. The Public Utilities Holding Company Act of 1935 required massive divestiture. Less well know is the far-reaching divestiture required by the Banking Act of 1933, which divorced investment banking and commercial banking. Likewise, the McKellar-Black Air Mail Act of 1934 forced General Motors to relinquish its interests in various airlines and aircraft manufacturers.

Areas where the legislative route may prove essential are the divorcement of large petroleum companies from other energy sources, the prohibition of certain kinds of joint ventures in the petroleum industry, and the divestiture of Western Electric from AT&T. These are matters that likely will never be accomplished by antitrust actions. The time seems ripe for the Congress once again to take direct action in bringing about a more competitive and decentralized economy.

Redirecting the FTC's Mission

The kindest thing many commentators often say about the FTC is that it's good to have some competition in antitrust enforcement. But this is more a criticism of the Antitrust Division than a justification for the FTC. To justify its existence (outside the consumer protection area) the FTC must do more than compete with and duplicate the Justice Department; it must return to its original mission.

Unhappily, the FTC has strayed far from its original

congressional mandate. It was created partly as a successor to the Bureau of Corporations, formed in 1903. Congress had given the commissioner of the bureau power to investigate the organization and competitive behavior of corporations and to publish reports for the Congress, the President, and the public.[17] An underlying premise for the bureau was that the public was entitled to know the facts of business affairs, because, as Theodore Roosevelt declared in his first inaugural, "The first requisite [of corporate accountability] is knowledge, full and complete; knowledge which may be made public to the world."

During 1913 and 1914 the Congress heatedly debated alternative ways of dealing with the increasing centralization of power that the Sherman Act had failed to stop. Out of this debate came the FTC Act of 1914 that created a new regulatory commission with enforcement and investigative missions. Its enforcement mandate required it to prohibit specific anticompetitive practices spelled out in the Clayton Act of 1914, as well as other practices that the FTC in its expertise judged to be "unfair methods of competition" under authority of section 5 of the Federal Trade Commission Act.

Its investigative responsibilities were to be an extension of those of the Bureau of Corporations.[18] Although it had the power to adjudicate practices its investigations found to be anticompetitive, the commission was fundamentally a fact-finding body. To accomplish this, section 6 of the FTC Act granted broad authority for undertaking investigations requested by the President and the Congress, or at the commission's own initiative.[19] Section 7 of the act provided that, upon direction of the courts, the commission serve as "a master in chancery, to ascertain and report an appropriate form of decree" in cases tried by the Department of Justice. Clearly, Congress perceived a different role for the FTC than the one it plays today.

In 1915 the staff of the Bureau of Corporations was

transferred to the FTC, which in its first years was composed predominantly of economists and accountants. During its first two decades the commission initiated and completed many broad investigations, often at the request of Congress, which frequently used the commission's investigative inquiries in framing legislation such as the Packers and Stockyards Act of 1921, the Grain Futures Act of 1922, the Radio Act of 1927, the Security Act of 1933, the Communications Act of 1934, the Public Utility Holding Company Act of 1935, the Federal Power Act of 1935, and the Robinson-Patman Act of 1938.

The commission's investigative function has assumed declining significance since the late 1930s. This was not because its legal authority was diluted. On the contrary, whereas the courts initially were hostile to the commission's authority to require special reports under section 6, in 1950 the Supreme Court settled the matter in the commission's favor.[20]

Why, then, the relative inaction of recent decades? Although various factors are responsible, a major reason has been the commission's preoccupation with legal matters. Much of its antitrust work has paralleled that of the Antitrust Division. Perhaps more fundamental has been the commission's weakening ties with the Congress and the President. Although the commission may have remained an independent agency, it also has been ignored. Neither Congress nor the President relies extensively on the commission for expertise about questions of market power and conduct.

A great potential exists, however, for the commission to return to its original mission. There seems to be a new mood in the White House and the Congress, as they struggle with complex questions of market power in the fields of energy and elsewhere.

The commission must do more than provide testimony concerning bills before the Congress. It must also conduct inquiries that will be useful in framing new legislation. It should on its own initiative, or at the request of the Congress, launch large-scale inquiries into matters that are simply too big and too complex for congressional staffs to undertake. It should also complement the Justice Department's enforcement policy, not duplicate it.

Such inquiries will require creating investigative groups consisting of economists, accountants, and lawyers. They must be of sufficient size and expertise to conduct a large-scale inquiry and to do legal battle, where necessary, with those who would resist investigation.

Success requires the support of the Congress, whose arm the FTC is supposed to be. It can be done with effective leadership and a commission that is courageous enough to support such leadership.

Complementing Incomes Policy with Procompetition Policies

At best, industrial restructuring and other procompetition efforts are long-run policies. There is a growing consensus among economists that one of the major costs of market power is that it worsens the tradeoff between unemployment and inflation.[21] The historical evidence is growing and—to me—is very persuasive.

The Kennedy and early Johnson years taught us that semivoluntary wage–price controls could be moderately successful in pushing toward full employment without triggering inflation. They could not, of course, cope with the Vietnam-caused inflation, which they were not designed or able to prevent.

President Nixon taught us additional lessons about the

market power–inflation problem. Flushed with victory, he embraced lustily an antiinflation policy based on the free market. The result: simultaneous inflation and unemployment, climaxing in the adoption of a hastily contrived wage–price control system. After this system was phased out, President Ford reaffirmed his faith in free markets by pursuing the time-honored laissez-faire policy of relying exclusively on monetary contraction to control inflation. The result was an even worse disaster. Despite the conscious and purposeful contraction of the economy, resulting in the highest unemployment rate since the 1930s, inflation lingered on.

What went awry? Did not orthodox economics teach that prices and wages would stop rising when factories and workers were idled as aggregate demand was contracted?

The trouble was not inelegance of economic theory. Rather, the trouble was that a theory that assumes the competitive world of Adam Smith does not serve in an economy where market power will not yield to restrictive monetary policies. The fatal flaw in most macroeconomic planning since World War II has been the assumption that free markets are sufficiently pervasive to discipline key price and wage decision makers. Had market forces been keenly competitive in all industries, as they are in many, the inflation would have moderated quickly in response to the monetary and fiscal restraints imposed in 1969 and again in 1974.

Though economists still debate these matters heatedly in the academic journals, those who are forced to cope with the problem have increasingly recognized that unless market power is dissipated or harnessed, it is impossible to achieve full employment without inflation. Even that steadfast disciple of laissez-faire economics and an architect of President Nixon's disastrous 1969–70 experiment with free markets, Dr. Arthur F. Burns, chairman of the Federal Reserve System, has come to recognize that market power makes it impossible to rely solely on macro policies. "Not a few of our corporations and trade unions," he has said, "now have the power to exact rewards that exceed what could be achieved under conditions of active competition. As a result, substantial upward pressure on costs and prices may emerge long before excess aggregate demand has become a problem." He therefore confesses that "managing aggregate demand," alone, "will not suffice to assure prosperity without inflation."[22]

The nexus between corporate power and inflation is complex. It is rooted in the structural characteristics and performance of modern capitalism. Perhaps as much as $50 billion of excess profits will be redistributed in 1977 from consumers to the holders of market power.[23] I agree with the growing number of economists and public policy officials who believe there is a behavioral link between high profits of corporations with market power and the wage demands of organized labor. Simply put, the inflation problem is intensified by a struggle over income distribution. This view is held by many economists of varying political persuasion who have been forced to deal with the problem of economic power outside the classroom.

Gardner Ackley, a member of the Council of Economic Advisors during 1962-68, sums up his position as follows:

> My vision of the type of inflationary process which now concerns us sees it as essentially the byproduct of a struggle over income distribution, occurring in a society in which most sellers of goods and services possess some degree of market power over their own wages or prices (in money terms). The extent of each firms's or union's power at any given time is affected

by structural and market factors; the manner in which the power is used is affected by perceptions of what is happening, and by political attitudes and social norms. . . . In my view, this model of an inflation-generating struggle to increase or protect income shares . . . provides a substantially meaningful description of wage and price behavior in a modern industrial economy.[24]

Murray L. Weidenbaum, Assistant Secretary of the Treasury in the Nixon administration, expresses a similar theme:

> The concern with income distribution can be a powerful mechanism for motivating greater use of potential influence over wage and price decisions. After all, why should a blue collar worker really worry about his wage increases exceeding the growth of productivity . . . when he believes that management is being overpaid, that white collar workers "loaf," and that stockholders are obtaining too large a share of the proceeds both of current income and capital gains?[25]

If these interpretations are correct, and I think they are, the entire market power–inflation problem is much more complex than simple economic models can explain. I am always amazed that those who see with great clarity how powerful labor unions may contribute to an inflationary spiral by demanding wage settlements that outstrip productivity increases (even when such settlements are designed entirely to catch up with inflation) are blind to the role that excess corporate power plays in the inflationary process. Such economists fail to recognize how the corporate power problem may influence the perceptions of labor as to what is fair and just. So long as some corporations are permitted to enjoy persistently excessive profits, labor unions cannot be expected to exercise restraint in the use of their power. It misses the point to argue that eliminating monopoly profits in a particular industry is not important in fighting inflation because it will not significantly affect the consumer price index. This ignores the reality that it is unreasonable, and in a democracy perhaps impossible, to expect some persons to exercise restraint unless there is a national policy that places limits on market power in all segments of the economy. Thus procompetition policies play the dual role of reducing the power of those who hold it and encouraging other holders of power to use it responsibly. For these reasons, antitrust and other procompetition policies are essential ingredients of any program that expects other holders of power not to abuse their power.

Given our current industrial structure, we need some form of incomes policy that involves voluntary or mandatory price, profit, and wage restraints in industries where business and labor hold considerable power. I emphasize, however, that procompetition policies can play an important role in determining both the scope and the effectiveness of such programs. They are, therefore, complements and not substitutes for effective macroeconomic planning to achieve full employment. To a degree, we have a choice: either enlarge the area of effective competition or enlarge the amount of government involvement in business pricing decisions.

The Multinational Corporation

The social control of corporate power is no longer a purely domestic affair. The large modern corporation has become a key mechanism for transferring technology, capital resources, and managerial know-how. Its operations transcend national boundaries, and often even ideology, in the pursuit of profits on a global scale. The huge modern corporation has become a multinational enterprise, often larger than many sovereign states, and may show allegiance to none.

The emergence of the multinational corporation (MNC) as the dominant force in international affairs is altering the structure of world markets, often in the image of the capital-exporting countries.[26] For example, the market structures of Brazil and Mexico in many ways reflect the structures of the home markets of United States multinational corporations.[27]

Wherever it operates in market economies, corporate power has the same structural origins. Research conducted for the Senate Foreign Relations Committee supports "the proposition that the sources and fruits of market power are universal phenomena, displaying remarkable similarities in different nations despite variations in the cultural and institutional environment in which private corporations operate."[28]

When MNCs hold great power and reap rich rewards, social control of such power inevitably becomes the legitimate concern of host nations. Because they are American based and often are viewed as the chief American presence in a foreign land, they become intimately tied to our public interest. Any friction between them and foreign governments may ultimately affect American foreign policy.

New solutions to resolve conflict must be found. Just as the large corporation is here to stay within our boundaries, so is the MNC a permanent fixture on the international scene. The public policy issue, therefore, is not whether or not to have MNCs but how to ensure that they work in harmony with our international interests.

We only dimly perceive what public policy should be toward MNCs because they have grown so vast and complex that public policy makers do not possess sufficient reliable knowledge to fashion appropriate policies. Traditional antitrust policy can only play a more limited role in controlling MNC power than it can in controlling corporate power in domestic markets.

Although I have no grand agenda for dealing with MNCs, I believe an essential first step in redressing the balance in public versus private authority is to require that all large corporations be federally chartered, as opposed to the current policy of state chartering, thereby explicitly recognizing the special public character of these corporations and imposing special responsibilities on them.[29] I shall not attempt to spell out the provisions of such charters here. One of the chief goals, however, is to provide a window into MNC affairs by requiring greater disclosure of their operations and, perhaps, by having publicly appointed members on their boards. Some may view this as an unwarranted intrusion of the domain of private corporations. They have come to this view because in recent times many Americans have been taught to equate rights of the private corporation with those that are guaranteed the individual. Too many people have forgotten what was self-evident to our forebears. Theodore Roosevelt summed it up well when he said: "Great corporations exist only because they are created and safeguarded by our institutions; it is therefore our right and our duty to see that they work in harmony with these institutions."

The Time for Reform Is Now

Although these are modest proposals—some will even say an apology for the status quo—many who consider themselves "practical" men will dismiss them as being politically unrealistic, arguing that this is not the day of reform.

Many economists will be among these "practical" men. When called for counsel on matters of reform, economists generally are a very cautious and conservative lot, an establishment of prudent and respectable persons seeking the applause of the established holders of political and economic power. Economists enjoy sharing the limelight with men of high office asking for advice. They soon learn that those who are most likely to be asked back for return engagements are those who appear respectable because their advice reduces to a consensus that departs little from the preconceptions of those who are being advised.

But I submit that the "practical" politicians and the "prudent" economists are out of touch with the views of the American people. There is a great, and growing, concern with the problems of economic power. Listen to what the people say when they are asked to express their views on these issues:

> "In many of our largest industries, one or two companies have too much control of the industry." Agree: 58% in 1965; 82% in 1975.

> "There's too much power concentrated in the hands of a few large companies for the good of the nation." Agree: 52% in 1965; 78% in 1975.

> "For the good of the country, many of our largest companies ought to be broken up into smaller companies." Agree: 37% in 1965; 57% in 1975.[30]

Although the people have expressed increasing concern with centralization of economic power, they have lost confidence in their government's ability to cope with the problem. Whereas in 1973, 60 percent of the people said "government regulation is a good way of making business more responsive to people's needs," by 1975 only 53 percent believed the government could do the job.[31] This may reflect the post-Watergate loss of confidence in government's ability to do anything right, but more likely it reflects the common belief that government is controlled by and run for special-interest groups, especially large corporations. Whereas in 1964, 27 percent of the people believed that the "government is pretty well run by a few big interests," by 1972 fully 53 percent of the people held this view.[32]

Given the mood of the people, a constituency for reform does exist. What is needed is a workable program and enough courageous private citizens and public officials who are determined to make this the generation of reform.

NOTES

1. W. F. Mueller, "Conglomerates: A Nonindustry," in W. Adams, ed., *The Structure of American Industry* (forthcoming).
2. Federal Trade Commission, *Staff Report on Corporate Mergers* (1969), pp. 332-397.
3. *Fortune*, June 1965, p. 194.
4. Ibid.
5. FTC, *Staff Report on Corporate Mergers*, pp. 458-472.
6. *Wall Street Journal*, March 26, 1969.
7. The author was an economic expert in the government's merger cases involving ITT. See also Willard F. Mueller, "The ITT Settlement: A Deal with Justice," *Industrial Organization Review* (Spring 1973), pp. 68-86.
8. *The International Telephone and Telegraph Company and Chile, 1970-71*, report to the Committee on Foreign Relations, U.S. Senate, by the Subcommittee on Multinational Corporations, Committee Print, June 21, 1973; Anthony Sampson, *The Sovereign State of ITT* (New York: Stein & Day), 1973.
9. Unpublished study updating W. F. Mueller, *The Celler-Kefauver Act: Sixteen Years of Enforcement*, report to the Antitrust Subcommittee, Committee on the Judiciary, House of Representatives, October 16, 1967.
10. Ibid.
11. Ibid.
12. Mueller, "The ITT Settlement."

13. See the testimony of Bruce W. Marion and Willard F. Mueller before the Joint Economic Committee, March 30, 1977.

14. Richard Hofstadter, "What Happened to the Antitrust Movement?" in Early F. Cheit, ed., *The Business Establishment* (New York: Wiley, 1966), p. 114.

15. See W. F. Mueller, testimony on the Industrial Restructuring Act before the Senate Subcommittee on Antitrust and Monopoly, U.S. Senate, March 27, 1973.

16. *U.S.* v. *Columbia Steel Co.*, 344 U.S. 495 (1948).

17. George Rublee, "The Original Plan and Early History of the Federal Trade Commission," *Proceedings of the Academy of Political Science*, 11 no. 4 (January 1926): 666-67.

18. The bill that was originally introduced in the House of Representatives gave the FTC no regulatory authority; it was "hardly more than an amplification of the existing Bureau of Corporations" (Rublee, "The Original Plan," p. 667).

19. Additional broad investigative authority was provided by section 9 of the act.

20. *U.S.* v. *Morton Salt*, 338 U.S. 632 (1950).

21. For the author's views, see Willard F. Mueller, "Industrial Concentration: An Important Inflationary Force," in H. J. Goldschmid, ed., *Industrial Concentration: The New Learning* (Boston: Little, Brown, 1974).

22. Testimony of Arthur F. Burns before the Joint Economic Committee, February 20, 1973.

23. This estimate is based on Scherer's estimate that about 3 percent of GNP would be redistributed in the form of monopoly profits in 1966. F. M. Scherer, *Industrial Market Structure and Economic Performance* (Chicago: Rand McNally, 1971), p. 409.

24. G. Ackley, "An Incomes Policy for the 1970's," *Review of Economics and Statistics*, 54 (August 1972): 218.

25. M. L. Weidenbaum, "New Initiatives in National Wage and Price Policy," *Review of Economics and Statistics*, 54 (August 1972): 213.

26. See John M. Connor and Willard F. Mueller, *Market Power and Profitability of Multinational Corporations*, report to the Subcommittee on Multinational Corporations, Committee on Foreign Relations, U.S. Senate (forthcoming).

27. Ibid.

28. Ibid.

29. For the author's views on corporate chartering, see W. F. Mueller, "Corporate Secrecy vs. Corporate Disclosure," in R. Nader and M. Green, eds., *Corporate Power in America* (New York: Grossman, 1972), pp. 111-130, and testimony on corporate secrecy before the Monopoly Subcommittee on Antitrust and Monopoly, Committee on Small Business, U.S. Senate, March 8, 1973.

30. The following are based on the findings of the Opinion Research Corporation, which prepares a "public opinion index" for its corporate clients. These findings were reported by Harry W. O'Neill, executive vice president, Opinion Research Corporation, to the Wisconsin Association of Manufacturers and Commerce, September 24, 1976.

31. Ibid.

32. University of Michigan Center for Political Studies, "Election Surveys," as reported in *The Crisis of Democracy*, report of the Trilateral Commission (New York: New York University Press, 1975).

The Great Recession of the 1970s: Domestic and International Considerations

Leonard A. Rapping*

PEOPLE WHO ARE burdened with the day-to-day activities of making a living are often slow to perceive momentous change. Professional economists are no exception. The long period of post–World War II prosperity has ended and the Great Recession of the mid-1970s has taken its place. In Western Europe, Japan, and the United States, over 20 million people are unemployed. Plants and machines are idle. The international commercial and financial economy is in disarray. Increasingly, we doubt the ability or, indeed, the will of the Government to reverse the ominous tide of events. As in the 1930s, economic stagnation both promotes and is promoted by international trade and financial disorder, a situation which constantly threatens to erupt into "trade war." These problems are exacerbated by an unprecedented transfer of wealth to the oligarchs of OPEC and the major oil companies. To finance the import of oil, as well as other commodities, the Third World countries, along with Britain and Italy,

---

*I wish to thank my many friends and colleagues who have shared their thoughts on the current crisis. Sam Bowles, James Crotty, and Charles Sackery have been especially helpful, but I alone must bear full responsibility for any excesses contained herein.

have accumulated massive debts, and in many cases their obligations exceed their ability to pay.

All of these events occurred since the breakdown of the Bretton Woods system in August of 1971. This breakdown has resulted in floating exchange rates which, when coupled with generalized recession, pose a constant threat that international commercial disintegration will occur and will deepen the recession. While international capitalists, under the aegis of the Trilateral Commission, seek to replace the Bretton Woods system with a new international monetary order, competitive pressures among the powerful capitalist states, as well as conflict between the Third World and the nations of the north, constantly threaten the successful implementation of the commission's proposals. International order is difficult to achieve among unequals, and no nation is sufficiently powerful to impose order unilaterally.

Historically, economic malaise breeds political change. In Italy, France, Spain, and Portugal, Communist and socialist parties gain in electoral strength, while at the same time right-wing movements respond. These political developments in Europe are reminiscent of the 1930s. In southern Africa, white rule is challenged. In large parts of Latin America and Asia, repressive military juntas destroy human rights—a practice that was common enough in the past but is now occurring with disquieting frequency. Pinochet, Marcos, Park, and Geisel have ended all democratic pretense in their parts of the capitalist world.

In the United States, the fiction of honesty and basic decency in government is exploded. Almost daily, corporate political abuse is disclosed. The increasing concentration of economic power manifests itself as corporate financial intervention in the political process, both at home and abroad. Elected and appointed public officials prostitute themselves for giant corporations and for foreign agents. Even a President must leave office because of political scandal. Government agencies, such as the FBI and the CIA, engage in illegal activities. The post-World War II order has ended.

The Spread of Pessimism

In this environment of domestic recession and international economic disorder, many are increasingly concerned that the uninspired economic recovery of 1975-76 portends economic and political malaise. Five years ago, the possibility of another deep descent of Great Depression proportions was unthinkable. But now there is a not insignificant number of people who see this possibility as less than remote. There is pessimism and growing fear in Western Europe that stagnation and austerity are the order of the day. This fear is reflected even in the strongest economy of the region, West Germany. Pessimistic talk is common among top advisors and West German industrialists. Chancellor Helmut Schmidt, evidencing uncharacteristic concern for the economic future, said in a New Year's Day message: "In the last few months it has become clear that things will never again be the way they were before 1974."

While Schmidt bemoans the end of an era, others concentrate on the signs of increasing economic and political turmoil. Lawrence Viet, an economist, writing recently in the prestigious journal *Foreign Affairs* (55, no. 2 [January 1977]: 263), has a section heading in an article on the "Troubled World Economy" titled "Doldrums or Depression?" He says: "The meaning of the latest economic indicators may be unclear, but at best they are signaling a pause in the economic recovery of the major industrialized nations and a new wave of political malaise." And Richard

Whalen, in a *Harper's* article titled "The Coming Crisis in Europe" (254, no. 1520 [January 1977]: 25), observes that "European capital has reacted to an increasingly hostile political climate by going on strike. . . . Even in Germany, the level of capital spending is no higher than it was five years ago."

Whether the Western capitalist system will plunge into another Great Depression or whether it will simply stagnate at high but politically tolerable levels of idle capacity and unemployment for an extended period of time is a prediction best left to the futurologists or the hucksters of depression-proof securities. For us, it is sufficient to recognize that just as laissez-faire capitalism failed in the 1930s, so the post–World War II version of limited welfare capitalism appears to have failed in the 1970s. The policies and tools of Keynesian demand management, which were an essential feature of the post–World War II era have either failed or have been renounced as the crisis of the 1970s has unfolded. Witness, if you will, the rather cautious proposals of the Carter administration to stimulate the economy.

Fiscal Policy in 1977

In 1974 the Republican administration announced, through a report issued by the Office of Management and Budget, that the 1970s would be years of high unemployment and economic stagnation. The new Carter administration, despite campaign rhetoric to the contrary, accepts this verdict. The Carter administration proposals for economic stimulation in the 1977 fiscal year—an $11 billion cut in personal income taxes, a $2 billion cut in corporate taxes, and a $2 billion increase in the various job programs—are not too dissimilar in dollar magnitude from what had been proposed by the outgoing Ford administration. With a recession-induced shortfall of national product of some $175 billion, the administration's proposals for economic stimulation appear more consistent with objectives of the Businessman's Roundtable or the Committee for Economic Development than with those of the AFL-CIO. Not unlike the early 1930s, the government conservatively responds to economic malaise. The principles of laissez-faire economics are in control at least temporarily.

The administration's policy is a modest one in which there is a plaintive hope that a mild stimulation of consumer spending will prop up stagnate corporate investment and generate a mild expansion. Some business tax cuts are thrown in, because the corporations demand them and because it is hoped that they will spur investment. But even under the best of circumstances this strategy is unlikely to "get the economy moving again."

The principal objective of capitalist governments is to protect the private enterprise system and to maintain the profits of the largest corporations. I will argue that rapid recovery and full employment are inconsistent with this objective, and that the administration's proposals are constrained by the incompatibility of full employment with the maximization of corporate profits. I do not wish to leave the impression, however, that the creation of full employment is a mystery. A massive program of public works would create full employment rather quickly, but it would destabilize the existing distribution of wealth and power in this nation. As Keynes wrote in 1940, "It appears to be politically impossible for a capitalist democracy to organize expenditure on a scale necessary to make the grand experiment which would prove my case except in war conditions."

Nevertheless, I recognize that within the guidelines of fiscal orthodoxy there is an important conflict in Washington over the way in which limited fiscal stimulation will be applied. Organized labor has for several years insisted on a heavier emphasis on direct job creation through public works rather than through the more indirect method of personal and business tax cuts, a method supported by the corporations as well as most professional economists. These proposals would be of benefit to working people, especially if the programs guarantee a decent wage and provide useful work. But to date, supporters of public works programs, training and youth programs, and public service programs have had limited success. As this political struggle proceeds, a public employment program with wage rates at the relief level might be acceptable to the corporate interests, especially if the program substitutes for extended unemployment compensation. However, even under these conditions such a program cannot assume functions that have traditionally been performed by the corporations. Any encroachment upon the domain of the corporations will produce intense resistance.

To accept a situation in which 8 to 12 million people are unemployed is to accept the associated social evils of unemployment: regional disparities in economic opportunity, burgeoning teenage prostitution, increased drug addiction and alcoholism, marital conflict, growing crime rates, and all the other social disorders associated with the inability of people to find work. Why, then, does the Carter administration refuse to push forward to full employment with all deliberate speed, even within the limits set by the existing institutions?

We are told that the threat of accelerating inflation is the constraint. At one level, and I fear at a somewhat superficial level, this is undoubtedly a correct understanding of capitalist dynamics. But it leaves unexplained the precise reasons why we should fear inflation more than unemployment. Undoubtedly, inflation per se is a problem, especially if the monetary and fiscal policies of the United States, Western Europe, and Japan are uncoordinated. But inflation is primarily a manifestation of underlying economic and social forces, the identification of which can provide us with an understanding far more instructive than if the matter is left at a level of analysis that obfuscates rather than clarifies. Let us turn to an examination of these forces, by which we will see that within the existing institutional limits the administration is "about as free as a slave crawling east on the deck of a slave ship sailing west," to quote David Caute.

The Boom of the 1960s: Setting the Stage for Stagnation

To understand the reasons why barriers to expansion now exist, it is necessary to understand that capitalist economies move inexorably from periods of prosperity to periods of recession and depression. This basic characteristic of capitalist dynamics was temporarily forgotten in the exuberance of prosperity during the period 1961 to 1969. Over these years, real output grew at an unprecedented rate of 5.5 percent per annum, while the reported unemployment rate fell from 6.7 percent of the labor force to 3.5 percent. This expansion characterized Western Europe as well as Japan, and world trade flourished. By the end of the period, Lyndon Johnson boasted, "No longer do we view our economic life as a relentless tide of ups and downs . . . no longer do we consider poverty and unemployment landmarks on our economic scene." But Johnson and his Keynesian advisors were wrong. Methodically and systemically, prosperity was sowing the seeds of its own destruction.

As unemployment and the threat of unemployment diminished, workers improved their position in the struggle over the social product. The "threat of the sack" no longer served to discipline workers. Profit margins deteriorated as workers improved their real wages at a rate faster than the growth in productivity. As profitability declined, corporations were increasingly dependent on debt as a means of financing their capital expenditures. There was enormous expansion in corporate debt. Meanwhile the international monetary system evidenced increasing signs of distress under the pressure of prosperity-induced worldwide inflation, which proceeded at uneven rates across countries and, in conjunction with other systemic forces, undermined the entire system of fixed exchange rates.

Labor's success in its direct confrontation with capital in the marketplace was reflected in the public sphere. Publicly funded social welfare programs were expanded. Medicaid, Medicare, Manpower programs, Community Action programs, and extensions in the Aid to Dependent Children program were some of the more noted successes. This relief explosion was not a direct result of prosperity. Rather, it resulted from mass protest. However, prosperity facilitated a liberal response from the government.

In the struggle over the social product, full employment and prosperity were to labor's advantage. Capitalists learned or relearned an old lesson: capitalism cannot stand full employment because the continuous decline in profit rates, profit shares, and the mass of profits would spell euthanasia of the capitalist class. From their perspective, the solution to the problem was unemployment and recession. In the perverse rationality of capitalist dynamics, recession was the rational way of dealing with the contradiction. But the necessary recession of 1969-70 was not permitted to run its painful course. Wage and price controls were introduced. Upon this weak foundation, there were two years of expansion. As the control program became increasingly contradictory, it was abandoned.

The Recession of 1973

In late 1973 another recession began, which has produced unemployment rates that are the highest workers have experienced since the late 1930s. Were it not for two consecutive record-breaking federal deficits in 1975 and 1976—$75 billion and $65 billion respectively—the situation would have been even more serious, for these deficits maintained the flow of income and provided liquid assets to the corporate sector. The mini-recovery from March of 1975 through the first three quarters of 1976 was disappointing for workers.

Real wages grew slowly although workers' productivity rapidly advanced. Consequently, as in the early stages of previous economic advances, profit margins were rapidly expanding. The reality and threat of unemployment performed its historic role, to squeeze labor. If the government were significantly to reduce the unemployment rate through massive monetary and fiscal stimulus, the fear of unemployment would no longer discipline labor and capital would find its profits threatened. It is for this reason that capital demanded fiscal restraint. For this and other reasons, to be explored in a moment, private capital investment in plant and equipment was stagnant. Without rapidly growing markets, investment will continue to stagnate. But without significant government stimulus, markets are unlikely to expand. Such are the contradictions of capitalist accumulation.

The struggle over real wages is mirrored in the struggle over publicly provided social services. Capital not only wants fiscal restraint, it wants its taxes cut. Lower corporate taxes mean higher after-tax profits, and restrictive monetary and fiscal policies mean more unemployment, hence lower real wages and consequently higher profits. This twin objective results in a growing insistence that publicly provided social services be reduced. Nowhere is this so clear as in states such as New York and Massachusetts, where a major assault on public employment and public relief has been proceeding for almost three years.

I have argued that the threat of rising real wages is a constraint on capital investment. There are also other constraints worth considering. Consistent with previous business cycles, the mild expansion over the previous seven quarters has led to rapidly improving corporate profits. In the first quarter of 1975, corporate profits were $54 billion, while in the third quarter of 1976 they had risen to about $85 billion, up 57 percent. Over the same period, corporate profits before taxes, plus depreciation reserves (a measure of cash flow), have risen approximately 41 percent. The development of large-scale unemployment followed by a slow recovery has worked to capital's advantage, as measured by profit flows, and as one would predict from the class-struggle theory I have outlined. But unlike previous post–World War II expansions, the corporations have failed to reinvest these profits in expanding their plant and equipment. This failure is reflected in the statistics on capital spending. Despite the severity of the decline in expenditures for nonresidential structures and producers' durable equipment in late 1973 through early 1975, these expenditures have been unusually sluggish during the recent recovery, increasing by only 1.7 percent per annum. This lack of strength in corporate investment is reminiscent of the years 1933 to 1937, a period when capital expenditures stagnated and prevented the growth in production and employment necessary to fully revive the economy from the depths of the Depression reached in 1933. Not until World War II did the depression of the 1930s end.

Historically, periods of economic stagnation give rise to the argument that the phenomenon is secular and that the possibilities of capitalist expansion have been exhausted. John Stuart Mill made the argument in the 1870s; Alvin Hanson, an American Keynesian, for reasons different from Mill, made the argument in the 1930s; and Paul Sweezy, an American Marxist, asserts the argument in the 1970s. Undoubtedly, there are important elements of insight in these arguments, each of which differs in essential details. However, in the 1970s it is unnecessary to argue that the absence of either epoch-making innovations or a slowdown in the rate of population expansion accounts for the present predicament.

Instead, the situation can be explained by an argument based on systemic cyclical instability rooted in the struggle between capital and labor over the disposition of the social product. Within this framework, we can account for the failure of investment over the past two years. We need not appeal to stagnation theory. I have already discussed the role of potential real-wage increases. Let us now consider corporate debt.

Corporate Debt and the Stagnation of Real Nonresidential Fixed Investment

The expansion of the 1960s, temporarily interrupted in 1969-70 but given added life by the Nixon-imposed price controls of 1971-73, was, to an unprecedented extent, debt fueled. Corporate debt tripled in fifteen years. Consumer debt soared. State and local governments borrowed heavily, with New York City being one of the more widely publicized casualties of this process. Twice, the Central Bank attempted to abort the process, once in 1966 and again in 1970, but on both occasions the bank relented for fear of precipitating a financial panic which would not only threaten the survival of many corporations but would have unforeseen but potentially disastrous consequences for production.

By 1974 this frenzied process of debt creation reached the point where both the commercial banks and the nonfinancial corporations had developed liquidity problems, as reflected in "fragile" balance sheets. In the nonfinancial corporate sector, about 55 percent of capital spending was being financed by external funds. This figure stood at only 25 percent in the early 1960s. An increasing fraction of profits was required to service the resulting debt. The interest coverage ratio, defined as pretax income plus interest expense divided by interest expense, fell from about 12 in 1964 to only 3 in mid-1974. Meanwhile, the commercial banks themselves were increasingly exposed. The loan to deposit ratio, for example, rose from about 50 percent in 1961 to over 75 percent in mid-1974. This process of credit expansion was unsustainable and ended with the sharp decline in industrial production in the fourth quarter of 1974.

No single factor can fully account for a process as complicated as that of capital accumulation fueled by the creation of debt. I have seen it argued that a preference for outside financing develops because of the federal corporate tax laws which permit interest to be "expensed" while profits are taxed. While undoubtedly relevant, this consideration does not provide an adequate explanation of the phenomenon. More convincing is the argument that, in the struggle over the social product, labor was increasingly successful after 1965 as the reserve of unemployed labor was depleted. Price increases, that is, inflation, were insufficient to maintain profitability, however measured, and debt financing was required to maintain desired rates of investment. Again we see that full employment creates contradictions which, within the logic of capitalist dynamics, seek resolution through the process of recession, depression, and unemployment.

The excessive debt and illiquidity that developed during the expansion of the 1960s and again in the early

1970s—a situation alarmingly discussed in the special issue of *Business Week* titled "The Debt Economy" (October 1974)—has been reduced but not eliminated by the Great Recession that began in late 1973. Increased corporate profits have been used to retire debt, to restructure debt, to acquire cash reserves, and to acquire Treasury bills and notes. The huge federal deficits of 1975 and 1976 have been absorbed in large part by the financial and nonfinancial corporations. Nevertheless, the balance sheets of these institutions remain precariously illiquid, at least by early 1960s standards. For example, the loan to deposit ratio of commercial banks has fallen only slightly from its late 1974 peak, which, at that time, was generally viewed as excessively high. Similarly, since the spring of 1975 nonfinancial corporate cash flow has greatly improved and funds have been used to improve their financial affairs; they have repaid bank loans, greatly reduced their short-term debts, and added to their cash reserves. But these institutions still remain less liquid and more debt ridden than they were in the early 1960s. The interest coverage ratio, for example, rose from its mid-1974 level of 3 to a little over 6, but it remains well below its early 1960s level. Previously accumulated debt remains a constraint on capital accumulation.

The restraining influence of debt has not gone unnoticed. In a recent American Assembly publication, Reginald Jones, chairman and chief executive officer of General Electric Company, asserts: "As the result of excessive debt and the drying up of internally generated funds, corporate balance sheets place . . . restraints on corporate investments." Jones, echoing the current demand of corporate officials, goes on to argue for corporate tax cuts, the removal of "government mandated pollution controls" and, in a somewhat indirect way, the reduction in publicly provided social services, another current objective of corporate officialdom.

The slow and tortuous process of eliminating the excessive accumulation of nonfinancial corporate debt represents yet another example of the functional role of recession. The debt accumulation of the 1960s and early 1970s, like the increase in real wage rates during that period, has been a barrier to expansion. Yet it should be clear that excessive debt and the potential of rising real wages are not the only barriers to expansion. The low level of capacity utilization, a result rather than a cause of recession, is obviously a barrier to private accumulation. And it should be added that other less tangible but equally important considerations are relevant. The collapse of the international monetary system, political turmoil in Western Europe and the Third World, the increase in the relative price of energy, and other events of this tumultuous decade have undoubtedly left their mark on what we might term "business confidence."

The administration's efforts to steer a cautious course, coupled with those of the Central Bank, are fraught with risk. The economy is too unstable for a prudent person to exclude the possibility of an unexpected but sharp decline in output. In such an event, the shocks sent through the system could have disastrous implications. I have in mind, for example, problems associated with the continuing debt overhang. With an absolute decline in business activity, default on a large scale is a distinct possibility. Admittedly, the Central Bank, working in tandem with the large commerical banks as well as the Federal Deposit Insurance Corporation, aborted a financial panic in late 1974 and early 1975 by its lender-of-last-resort activities. Can we be certain that it will succeed again? Bankers and public officials make mistakes or misjudge situations. Witness the number of past and present administration officials who allege that the government's financial, political, military, and moral disaster in Indochina can be explained by a series of unfortunate mistakes.

Prospects for the Future

Capitalism cannot tolerate full employment, nor can it tolerate economic inertia, indefinitely. A long period of intolerable unemployment rates raises the prospect of heightened class conflict in the United States just as it did in Britain during the stagnant years of the 1920s. The prospect of labor unrest is already indicated by events in the miners', steel workers', and machinists' unions. The more dramatic labor unrest in Western Europe indicates the political infeasibility of a slow recovery. Moreover, under conditions of gradual and uneven expansion, the servomechanism is too uncertain to eliminate the possibility of a sharp decline in industrial production. This would create unpredictable social and political developments.

The possibility of a "social contract" to serve as the basis of a noninflationary expansion is a faint hope in light of the unsuccessful application of wage-price controls in both Western Europe and the United States in the past decade. Experiments might occur, but without an event such as America's entry into World War II, which mobilized an entire nation, or barring the emergence of an authoritarian government, as in Nazi Germany during the 1930s, it is difficult to imagine that labor would voluntarily submit to legislative restrictions on its right to bargain collectively over wages and working conditions. Yet without wage and price controls, the application of Keynesian fiscal stimulus is impossible. Indeed, under economic conditions such as those of the present, fiscal stimulus has never been tried on a massive scale without controls.

Moreover, without the introduction of extensive microplanning, a permanent system of wage-price controls is untenable. This suggests that the contradictions of the current period are likely to be resolved by the slow and inexorable development of increased central planning. This historical process may be temporarily arrested by unpredictable events; it may even seem less likely tomorrow than it does today; but it is clearly the direction in which the system is moving.

Already there are developments in the structure of industry that indicate the centralization of capital, a process which might facilitate centralized planning. Primarily through mergers, the 200 largest conglomerate nonfinancial corporations now control over 65 percent of industrial assets. In 1947 this figure was 42 percent. In the energy field, the Seven Sisters have monopolized the production and distribution of oil, coal, and natural gas. In banking, the process of centralization is proceeding at an even faster pace. In 1969 the share of deposit liabilities of the 100 largest banks was 48 percent, while in 1974 this figure was 70 percent. The five largest banking organizations now hold 25 percent of all deposits. Directorships between these giant banks and giant conglomerate corporations are closely interlocked. Representatives of these industrial and financial giants dominate the decision-making bodies of the Central Bank and hold key cabinet positions. While these developments create a framework for central planning, they are not without internal contradictions. Capital is not a monolith, and internal dissension remains. If central planning is to come, there will be a struggle over the control of the planning process. Labor and its allies need not be passive.

International Considerations

The requirement for domestic economic planning is paralleled by the need for international planning. To understand the current international economic and political situation, a brief review of certain historical events will be instructive. We might then judge the extent to which international planning is required and the prospects for its achievement in the foreseeable future.

Great Britain provided order for the capitalist world in the nineteenth century. With its financial and military dominance, its corporations penetrated many parts of the world. Through a system of colonial governments, British capitalists exploited subject peoples and the resulting profits were used to expand British capital on an ever enlarging scale. But the profitability of the British colonial system attracted imitators and competitors from France, Germany, and the United States. Increasingly, Britain's industrial supremacy decayed, and by the end of World War I it was no longer able to provide order and stability in the commercial and financial relations among the capitalist nations. Without a hegemonic power to serve as the enforcer of intracapitalist order, trade relations among the capitalist countries were unstable in the 1920s, and disintegrated when production collapsed in the 1930s. There followed a great war in which the factories of Europe were destroyed and a good part of an entire generation of young Europeans was killed or mutilated. Because of its geographic advantage and the momentum of its growing economic power, the United States emerged from this traumatic experience as the world's leading industrial power. At the Bretton Woods conference of 1944 the United States dictated the post–World War II financial and commercial order for the non-Communist world. Exchange rates were stabilized and the United States dollar was to serve as both an international money and a reserve currency. New York firmly replaced London as the financial center of the capitalist world. A system of free trade and the free flow of capital was erected on the foundation of the Bretton Woods agreement. Under American dominance, international lending agencies such as the International Monetary Fund and the World Bank were established.

Within this order, the United States accelerated its penetration of the European and Japanese empires. In Latin America, Africa, Europe, and Asia, the United States established a system of military bases designed to maintain access to cheap raw materials, to provide secure markets, to support friendly governments, and to provide military security for the expansion of its multinational corporations. Governments amenable to American economic penetration were the recipients of economic and military assistance. Governments which were not amenable were overthrown. For example, in the 1950s governments that were unfriendly to the United States, in Iran and Guatemala, were overthrown, while in the 1970s a similar event occurred in Chile. Under this neocolonial system, the direct investments of United States multinational corporations grew from about $10 billion at the end of World War II to upward of $150 billion in 1971. A large export surplus and the willingness of foreign central banks to hold dollars facilitated the accumulation of these assets.

This global expansion did not go unnoticed at home, but those who might have articulated opposition to United States policy in the post–World War II period were discredited, blacklisted, interrogated, humiliated, and often denied access to a livelihood by an anti-Communist crusade fronted by a senator from Wisconsin and a congressman from California. Just as the "white man's burden" was a cover argument for British imperialism, anti-communism was a cover for United States imperialism.

Within the framework of *Pax Americana,* world trade grew rapidly. Eventually, Western Europe and Japan became viable economic competitors of the United States. Increasingly, United States industrial leadership decayed. These countries, which were becoming important capitalist rivals, benefited from the order created by the United States, but their growth also contributed to the collapse of that order. And other forces were undermining the

Bretton Woods system as well. The Soviet Union grew more powerful. Third World revolutionary forces were difficult and expensive to contain. Finally, the defeat of the United States government in Indochina signaled momentous changes in the economic and political order which the United States had established. These varied historical forces manifested themselves in the collapse of the Bretton Woods system in August of 1971. The United States was no longer capable of unilaterally enforcing order on the world capitalist system.

With floating exchange rates replacing fixed exchange rates, international cohesion was undermined, as it had been once before in the period between World War I and World War II. Fixed exchange rates provide the advantages of a common currency, while floating rates are unstable and are an invitation for governments, motivated by mercantilist aspirations, to manipulate the exchange rate. The demise of the Bretton Woods system not only cut exchange rates loose, but also threatened the commercial policy of free trade, so carefully erected by the United States after World War II. The dwindling trade surplus of the United States, which was partially responsible for the collapse of the Bretton Woods agreement, was also responsible for the United States' drive to export grains with the inevitable effect of an increase in domestic food prices. Also, all the forces which weakened United States control were partially responsible for the emergence of OPEC and the staggering increase in energy prices. Finally, these same historical forces, coupled with profit squeezes and debt accumulation, are important in understanding the Great Recession of 1973. These recessionary forces gathered considerable momentum in late 1974 and early 1975 when industrial production declined by 28 percent. Simultaneously, precipitous declines in production occurred in Western

Europe and Japan. The resulting worldwide recession, coupled with the earlier collapse of international financial order, threatens the cohesiveness of international trade relations.

International Instability: Commercial Relations

While no two historical periods are exactly alike, there is some similarity between the current period and the period between the two world wars.

Under the pressure of declining production and ensuing financial panic, the solidarity of international monetary and trade relations collapsed in the early 1930s. Competitive devaluations, import restrictions, exchange controls, and other protectionist policies represented desperate, and ultimately unsuccessful, attempts by nations to insulate their economies from the destructive economic forces that were everywhere gathering momentum. International chaos undoubtedly contributed to the descent into the abyss. The breakdown of the fragile international order of the 1920s was an important factor contributing to both the severity and the duration of the Great Depression and to the rise of fascism in Europe.

While international trade and financial relations among industrialized capitalist countries have not yet deteriorated to the level of chaos reached in the early 1930s, stresses and strains are everywhere in evidence. The protectionist trend initiated by the breakdown of the Bretton Woods system in August of 1971 was heightened by the trade deficits that Western Europe and Japan developed vis-à-vis the oil-exporting countries after the historic increase in oil prices in the fall of 1973. Perhaps even more important in stimulating protectionist attitudes and policies has been the onset of recession in late 1973 and early 1974 in Western Europe, the United States, and Japan. Although not entirely synchronized, the forces of recession spread rapidly. Unemployment rates rose quickly in Britain, Italy, France, West Germany, Japan, and elsewhere. The recovery of 1975-76 has been too weak to significantly affect the widespread unemployment among the industrialized capitalist countries. Conditions are especially bad in Britain, Italy, and France.

In response to trade deficits and unemployment, countries have manipulated their exchange rates in an attempt to ameliorate these problems. Australia and New Zealand, for example, openly devalue their currencies, while there is constant suspicion that Japan (and probably others) covertly manipulate the yen to stimulate exports, and while Italy imposes taxes on all foreign currency transactions to limit imports and to control the movement of short-term capital abroad.

The movement of currency values is only one reflection of international instability. More direct commercial conflict is in evidence. The determined Japanese export drive, which has indeed generated substantial trade surpluses for that country, has prompted a protectionist response in Western Europe, while the United States is warning the Japanese to go slow on their exports of automobiles, television sets, steel, and other items to the United States. The most recent manifestation of the European Economic Community's growing concern over Japanese exports has been the imposition of duties on the import of Japanese ball and roller bearings. While this restriction of trade prompted the Japanese to promise to limit the export of merchant ships that are competitive with those produced in Western Europe, the tensions remain high, in considerable part because the competitors are afflicted by economic recession.

Western Europe has tensions with the United States as well. Most recently, West Germany concluded a $5 billion trade arrangement with Brazil which involved the sale of nuclear reactors and plants for processing nuclear materials. The United States objected on the grounds that such sales are not in the mutual interest of the United States and West Germany, but the Germans went ahead despite American protests. Similar conflict exists between the United States and France. The latter's effort to sell nuclear power plants has met with American resistance, just as Concorde landing rights have created a further source of friction.

Even before the onset of recession and the increase in the price of oil, France, Great Britain, and Italy had experienced difficult economic problems. But now their problems disarticulate the European Economic Community, and there is considerable evidence that Western Europe is in disarray. In these three countries there are excessive balance of payment deficits, high unemployment rates for the first time in decades, rapidly depreciating currencies, and slow growth of national product. All of these events signal a growing apart between these countries and the rest of the Common Market countries, led by West Germany. While West Germany is recessed and unemployment rates are high, its rate of inflation is only 5 percent, compared to Italy and Great Britain's 20 percent and 16 percent respectively. West Germany's balance of payments is in surplus and its growth in national product, while not high, has, until recently, been respectable.

The disparities that have developed make it increasingly contradictory for Italy and Great Britain to remain constrained by the requirements of Common Market membership. There is more evidence of class conflict now than in recent years, as the governments of these countries pursue policies to reduce the rate of inflation and to reduce real wages. As a condition for loans from the International Monetary Fund, Great Britain has increased taxes and reduced social services. In addition, the Labor party government's "social contract" with the Trade Union Congress curbed wages at 4.5 percent per annum. With inflation rates now running in the neighborhood of 15 percent, the purchasing power of the wages of the average British worker has fallen by 20 percent. It is unlikely that organized labor will continue to accept voluntary restraint on money wages. There might well be what Chancellor of the Exchequer Denis Healy fears most: "the anarchy of strikes." Attempts by the government and the International Monetary Fund to facilitate the reintegration of Britain into the Common Market by attempting to reduce inflation rates, and successfully reducing real wage rates, exemplify the social conflict occasioned by the present instability in international economic affairs.

These events in the international sphere are surprisingly reminiscent of the 1930s. There is political disorder and the ever present threat of "trade war." Under these circumstances, perhaps it is not so surprising that capitalists in the United States refuse to accumulate physical assets. After all, most accumulation is undertaken by multinational corporations that coordinate the investment strategies of their subsidiaries. When there is political and economic instability in various parts of the world it might be best to accumulate financial rather than physical assets and await the possible reestablishment of international stability.

The deficit-ridden countries, France, Britain, and Italy, need the export markets of West Germany and the United States. They are beseeching these countries to expand their economies. But the fiscal and monetary authorities of the United States and West Germany, fearful of inflation and rising real-wage rates, and convinced that their economies must be purged of the excesses from the previous decade, are unresponsive. Like the United States, West Germany is pursuing conservative fiscal and monetary policies; indeed, so are the Japanese. The conservative economic thinking of Friedrich Hayek, dominant in the early 1930s, has reemerged in the mid-1970s. Except by the painful process of internal adjustment, these countries have no option. In refusing to provide export markets for these deficit-ridden countries, the United States and West Germany are insisting that these governments deflate their economies.

In the United States and West Germany, policies designed to maintain high levels of unemployment are feasible because of the current absence of labor militancy. But in Italy, Great Britain, and France such policies are an invitation to class conflict. Loans from the commercial banks and the International Monetary Fund may be used to strengthen the backbone of these governments to resist in the struggle against their workers. This strategy on the part of the United States, with its junior partner West Germany, might ultimately create chaos and the demise of Center governments in these countries. Moreover, a cooperative policy of restraint is risky because unexpected declines in production can occur, and if this happens, an international financial panic might ensue which would exacerbate the decline in production.

International Instability: Debt Relationships

Since the late 1960s a virtual explosion of lending has occurred in what is called the Eurodollar market. These loans have been extended by American and, to a lesser extent, European multinational banks to governments, individuals, and corporations. In addition to these private loans, there has been lending activity by such international agencies as the International Monetary Fund and the World Bank, as well as governments, mostly to governments. All of this lending activity has created a situation in which repayment is increasingly beyond the economic capacity of the debtors, especially when economic conditions are stagnant in the industrialized, capitalist countries. The problem has been exacerbated since 1973, when oil price increases, coupled with recession in the industrialized, capitalist nations, have required massive credits to finance the import deficits of Third World countries, as well as Great Britain and Italy. Over the past three years, much of this credit has been provided by multinational commercial banks that, in the parlance of the business, have been recycling "petrodollars."

While the source and terms of future credit extensions remain a conflict-ridden problem between debtors and creditors, a problem is also raised by the sheer magnitude of the existing debts relative to the ability of debtors to repay. Already, a few countries—Argentina, Zaire, and North Korea—are in de facto default. In the coming years a rising wave of defaults is likely. Regardless of the political forces of resolution set in motion by such events— stretchout, moratorium, foreign aid, deferral, negotiated reduction—the process is necessarily slow and highly destabilizing. Moreover, just as with the use of domestic negotiated settlements between the large commercial banks and the Real Estate Investment Trusts to forestall financial panic in the United States, any international solution short of reducing or eliminating the debts offers an inducement for the banks to repeat their abuses on an ever enlarging scale.

Of course, the problem of international debt which either cannot or will not be repaid is not a new phenomenon. In the period from 1918 to 1932, for example, numerous international conferences were required to negotiate the settlement of both the German reparations problem and the United States war debt problem. The stringent conditions imposed on the Germans was a source of both military and economic conflict during the period from the end of World War I to the Great Depression.

The French invaded the Ruhr over this issue, and the futile effort to collect sizable reparations was a factor in destabilizing intra-European commercial and financial relations during this period. German transfers contributed to the German hyperinflation of 1923, and the insistence on the repayment of international debts without regard to the underlying productive capacities of the countries involved hindered the achievement of international financial and trade stability during the 1920s.

International conflict between debtors and creditors is not by itself a sufficient cause of depression. But when it is added to the international instability caused by political uncertainty, gyrating exchange rates, and other forms of commercial disorder, it has the potential to trigger serious systemwide economic dislocations. Let us consider its potential.

The American multinational banks—for example, Citicorp, Chase, Morgan, Chemical—have engaged, in the aggregate, in many questionable lending activities over the past decade. Many Third World loans are but one example of these imprudent practices. Other examples include questionable commercial loans, many loans for tanker construction, loans to New York City, and the loans to the Real Estate Investment Trusts. Under these conditions, a series of defaults might initiate a run on Eurodollar deposits which, in the resulting race for "liquidity," might initiate what we frequently term a "panic" in international financial markets. A breakdown, if it eventually occurs, need not be confined to the banks; it might, but need not, paralyze the productive process. Whether the Central Bank of the United States could or would abort such an event is highly speculative. Much would probably depend on its ability to coordinate with the central banks of Europe. At present, no clear lines of authority exist. In any event, while some might be encouraged by the United States Central Bank's performance during the Penn Central crisis of 1971 and by its performance during the 1974–75 period, when it fulfilled its lender-of-last-resort mission, we might recall that it was either unable or unwilling to stem the tide of bank failure in the 1930–33 period.

The problems created by international debt extend beyond their potential impact on the international financial system. Any judgment concerning the potential for an international financial panic is necessarily speculative. But certainly the mere existence of the debt creates tensions between debtors and creditors. The debtors must export raw materials and other commodities to service the debt, and in some cases as much as 40 percent of the annual export earnings must be transferred to the creditors. This creates hostility and an interest in upsetting existing agreements. Moreover, when the creditor nations are depressed, exports cannot be sustained. In lieu of export markets, additional credits are required. Under these conditions, the large multinational banks and the International Monetary Fund are imposing stringent conditions on Britain, Italy, and Third World countries, conditions which are politically unpopular in the debtor nations. These interventions in the affairs of sovereign states are not dissimilar to events that occurred in New York City when the large commercial banks inserted themselves into the budgetary process of that city. It is rather ironic that tactics once reserved for people in the Third World are now being employed against the working class of Western Europe and the United States.

Conclusion

Renewed prosperity requires that the political and economic rivalries between the Western capitalist countries be contained by the reestablishment of an effective and widely accepted international control mechanism to replace the defunct mechanism that the United States established at Bretton Woods. An enforceable agreement on fixed exchange rates is required, and with such an agreement there is the need for a reconstituted International Monetary Fund. Equally important is the requirement for an effective General Agreement on Tariffs and Trade. Undoubtedly we will witness, as we did in the 1920s and 1930s, numerous international efforts at agreement on a new world economic system. The distribution of benefits among capitalists in the United States, Western Europe, and Japan is highly sensitive to the precise nature of the agreements reached. It is the prospect of gain which brings them together, but it is also the prospect of being disadvantaged that drives them apart.

There are specific problems whose resolution is enormously difficult. They include disposition of the existing Third World debt and how the losses from default will be distributed; the possibility of the remilitarization of West Germany and Japan; the dollar overhang problem; containment of the struggle for access to markets in Eastern Europe, China, and the Third World; access to raw materials and oil; coordination of internal fiscal and monetary policies; and integrating Britain and Italy into the new order. The mere listing of some of the required tasks indicates the enormity of the cooperative efforts that are called for.

The historical experience of the 1920s and 1930s suggests that intracapitalist rivalries are unlikely to be resolved by cooperation rather than conflict. In this event, the prospect of continued recession—perhaps even deep depression—would bring about prolonged human suffering and heightened class conflict. The future is uncertain, although there might eventually ensue a new epoch of capitalist prosperity—perhaps under fascism!

Contributors

Frank J. Bonello is an associate professor of economics at the University of Notre Dame. He has authored a book in the area of monetary economics and co-authored another in the area of economic education. He has published several articles in these two areas as well.

Kenneth P. Jameson is an associate professor of economics at the University of Notre Dame. Primarily a development economist, he has published widely, including articles in *Review of Economics and Statistics, Quarterly Journal of Economics,* and *Review of Politics.* In addition, he has held a Fulbright lectureship in Peru and has served as visiting professor in the Development Training Institute of the United States Agency for International Development.

Lawrence R. Klein, Benjamin Franklin Professor of Economics and Finance of the University of Pennsylvania, is president of the American Economic Association. He is also chairman of the board of trustees of Wharton Econometric Forecasting Associates, Inc., and principal investigator of Project LINK, an academically oriented research project linking econometric models of various regional and national economies. Dr. Klein served as coordinator for Jimmy

Carter's Economic Task Force during the 1976 presidential campaign. He is an internationally acclaimed author, speaker, and academician.

Willard F. Mueller is the William F. Vilas Research Professor of Agricultural Economics, and holds a professorship in both the Department of Economics and the Law School of the University of Wisconsin, Madison. He is the former chief economist and director of the Bureau of Economics for the Federal Trade Commission and the former executive director of the President's Cabinet Committee on Price Stability. In addition to providing expert testimony and economic advice to nearly a dozen U.S. congressional committees and agencies, Dr. Mueller has written widely in the area of antitrust and is perhaps the most respected U.S. economist in his specialty.

Leonard A. Rapping, professor of economics at the University of Massachusetts, is one of the best known political economists in the United States. He graduated, Phi Beta Kappa, from UCLA in 1956 and received his Ph.D. from the University of Chicago in 1961. He was on the editorial board of both the *American Economic Review* and *The Review of Radical Political Economy*. He has been a consultant to numerous federal agencies. Dr. Rapping has published extensively in the areas of labor economics, transportation economics, and macro economics. Presently, his special interest is the political economy of monetary and fiscal policy.

Thomas R. Swartz is an associate professor of economics and the director of the Notre Dame Center for Economic Education. He has served as a fiscal consultant for the President's Commission on School Finance, the Indiana Commission on State Tax and Financing Policy, and for numerous county and municipal agencies and departments. His research interests are in the area of state/local finance and economic education, where he has published widely.

Murray L. Weidenbaum is the director of the Center for the Study of American Business and the Mallinckrodt Distinguished University Professor of Washington University, St. Louis, Missouri. He currently serves as an adjunct scholar for the American Enterprise Institute for Public Policy Research, and formerly served as the assistant secretary of the Treasury for economic policy from 1969 to 1971 and an economist with the U.S. Bureau of the Budget from 1949 to 1957. Dr. Weidenbaum is a member of the boards of editors of the *Journal of Economic Issues, Publius, Journal of Federalism, Challenge, Magazine of Economic Affairs,* and of the board of economists of *Time.* His numerous books and professional articles have brought him wide recognition in the areas of public finance, defense economics, and industrial economics.

Charles K. Wilber is chairman and professor of economics at the University of Notre Dame. He is also adjunct senior staff associate, George Meany Center for Labor Studies and a member of the board of directors, Association for Evolutionary Economics. In addition to numerous articles in journals, he has published *The Soviet Model and Underdeveloped Countries* and *The Political Economy of Development and Underdevelopment.* His subject matter has ranged from Third World development through economic methodology to the role of the corporation in the American economy and in the current economic crisis.

LIBRARY OF DAVIDSON COLLEGE